JULIE WRIGHT

WHAT'S OUR Response?

Creating Systems and Structures
to Support ALL Learners

© Copyright 2021 by FIRST Educational Resources, LLC
Julie Wright
What's Our Response?
Creating Systems & Structures to Support ALL Learners
All rights are reserved. No part of this publication may be reproduced in any form or by any electronic or mechanical means, including information storage and retrieval systems, without permission in writing by FIRST Educational Resources, LLC. For information regarding permissions, please contact FIRST Educational Resources, LLC at info@firsteducation-us.com.

Published by:
FIRST Educational Resources, LLC
Winneconne, Wisconsin
www.firsteducation-us.com
info@firsteducation-us.com
ISBN: 978-1-7332390-3-5

Printed in the United States of America
(EnvisionInk Printing Solutions, Neenah, WI)

ABOUT THE AUTHOR

Julie Wright is a teacher, instructional coach, and educational consultant with more than 25 years of experience in rural, suburban, and urban education settings. She co-authored *What Are You Grouping For? How to Guide Small Groups Based on Readers—Not the Book* (Wright & Hoonan, 2019). Julie is best known for helping schools build capacity by matching their pedagogical beliefs to best practices. She holds National Board Certification as well as a Bachelor of Science in education, a Master of Arts in language arts and reading, K-12 reading endorsement, and a pre-K through grade 9 principal license from Ohio State University. In her free time, Julie loves walking, hanging out with family and friends, spending time in her garden, and she is a wannabe beekeeper. For more information about Julie, visit her website at www.juliewrightconsulting.com.

DEDICATION

This book is dedicated to Sydney, Noah, and Max.
Thanks for teaching me how to respond every day!

CONTENTS

Foreword	viii
Introduction	1
A Brief Historical Look at Time in Schools	3
Solving the Time Dilemma	4
This I Believe	5
Problems of Practice	5
How is This Book Organized?	8
Ready, Set, Let's Go!	8
Chapter 1	11
Problem of Practice #1: We Need to Break Out of the RtI Box.	11
Naming the Problem	13
Problem of Practice #1: We Need to Break Out of the RtI Box.	13
How the RtI Triangle Has Boxed Us In	15
Frequency, Intensity, Duration	16
Menu of Support Options	18
Reopening Old Wounds	21
Overproduction of Educational Products	21
This I Believe	22
What Can We Do About It?	22
Data Models are Only as Good as Our Assumptions	23
Remember the 8th Grade Team?	24
Defining Frequency, Duration, Intensity Protocol	27
Creating a Menu of Support Protocol	30
Sizing Up Our "Wealth" Protocol	38
Teacher Self-Reflection Protocol: Breaking Out of the RtI Box	40
Chapter 2	43
Problem of Practice #2: We Need to Honor and Increase Teacher Autonomy and Agency.	43
Naming the Problem	45
Problem of Practice #2: We Need to Honor and Increase Teacher Autonomy and Agency.	45

What are Autonomy and Agency?	45
This I Believe	46
Areas of Autonomy and Agency	46
What Can We Do About It?	51
Questions that Inspire Inquiry Protocol	52
Taking Stock of Our Autonomy & Agency Protocol	53
Taking Stock of Students' Needs & Wants Protocol	55
Individual Student Observation Template	57
Creating a Think Tank for Teachers to Study Protocol	58
If/Then Protocol	61
Teacher Self-Reflection Protocol: Autonomy & Agency	62

Chapter 3 — 65

Problem of Practice #3: We Need Child Study Teams Focused on Students' Assets.	65
Naming the Problem	67
Problem of Practice #3: We Need Child Study Teams Focused on Students' Assets.	67
Have We Created a Deficit-Focused Data Culture?	68
This I Believe	70
Going From Deficit-Based to Asset-Based	70
What Can We Do About It?	75
Data Meetings Focused on Action Steps Forward Protocol	78
Meetings Focused on an Inquiry Versus Deficit Stance Protocol	79
Roaming in the Known & the Wonderings Protocol	81
What Are Students Up to? Protocol	82
What Are Students Up to?	82
Reflecting—Naming—Reflecting Protocol	83
Do More / Do Less Protocol	84
Do More / Do Less	84
Assessing & Responding to Student Numeracy Data Protocol	85
Assessing & Responding to Student Numeracy Data Template	86
Assessing & Responding to Student Literacy Data Protocol	89
Assessing & Responding to Student Literacy Data Template	90

Teacher Self-Reflection Protocol: Asset-Based Child Study Teams	93

Chapter 4 — 95

Problem of Practice #4: We Need to Increase Students' Thinking and Doing Time	95
Meet Madison	96
Naming the Problem	98
Problem of Practice #4: We Need to Increase Students' Thinking and Doing Time	98
This I Believe	99
Closing the Gap Between Beliefs and Practices	99
What Can We Do About It?	102
Building on Successes	103
Studying Instructional Time Protocol	105
Planning for Student Work Protocol	107
Looking at Student Work Protocol	110
Closing the Gap Between Beliefs and Practices Protocol	114
Teacher Self-Reflection Protocol: Increasing Students' Thinking and Doing Time	117

Chapter 5 — 119

Problem of Practice #5: We Need Good Instruction Because that Makes the Best Interventions.	119
Efficient & Effective	121
Naming the Problem	123
Problem of Practice #5: We Need Good Instruction Because that Makes the Best Interventions.	123
Meet Jeffrey & Faduma	124
This I Believe	128
Bridging the Known to the New	128
What Can We Do About It?	129
Increasing Reading & Writing Volume	129
Early Intervention	135
Small Group Learning	138
Create Culturally Responsive Learning Opportunities	141
If-Then-So Process Protocol	143

Least Restrictive Environment Protocol	144
Increasing Reading and Writing Volume Protocol	145
Early Intervention Planning Protocol	147
Teacher Self-Reflection Protocol: Good Instruction Makes the Best Interventions	149
Chapter 6	**151**
Closing the Knowing-Naming-Doing Gap	151
Closing the Knowing-Naming-Doing Gap	155
A Call to Action	158
What's Our Response?	161
3 D's Protocol	163
Closing the Knowing-Naming-Doing Gap Protocol (Teachers)	164
Closing the Knowing-Naming-Doing Gap Protocol (Students)	165
Creating a Call to Action Protocol	166
Teacher Self-Reflection Protocol: Closing the Knowing-Naming-Doing Gap	167
References	**169**

FOREWORD

In 2004, three letters altered our intervention landscape. These letters known as RtI initially seemed to be promising. Yet, as countless schools implemented Response to Intervention, we have witnessed a steady decline in this promise as red flags continue to emerge. I detailed my RtI concerns in *RtI from All Sides: What Every Teacher Needs to Know* (2009, Heinemann). In her new book, *What's Our Response? Creating Systems and Structures to Support Students*, Julie Wright uses three letters of her own that illustrate a major RtI roadblock: "BOX." We must "break out of the RtI Box" that confine us in order to re-envision an RtI guided not by our homage to those combined letters but by our deep commitment to individuals that RtI should honor – our children.

Julie Wright shows us what this much needed shift in priorities could look like. She addresses the dangers of a constant bombardment of alluring quick fixes that reflect instructional and assessment boxes of our own. Julie doesn't just ask us to let go of what is not working but offers specific suggestions grounded in research and guiding beliefs about teaching and learning supported by reflective charts that provide a visual paper trail to change. Through Julie's wise advice based on her work in schools we learn steps that could transform "response" into "responsive" so that we can refocus on the children who depend on us to keep them at the center of all we do.

Julie gives us a front row view of her tireless work with teachers that can engage us in hard conversations about *What was* and *What is* so that we can contemplate *What could be*. She models how we can turn our thinking inward in ways that will alter an RtI deficit-focused data culture riddled with numerical laden spreadsheets to label students and justify pull out interventions and shows us an asset-based process designed to view children in terms of their strengths and the day-to-day assessments that can help us to uncover and celebrate those strengths. As a result, she helps us explore approaches that would shorten or even make unnecessary alternate intervention spaces so that we can at last reclaim our first line of defense: the classroom teacher.

It is my privilege to write this foreword and publicly endorse Julie Wright's wonderful book, *What's Our Response?* I am grateful for her thoughtful advice that will illuminate what really matters in any intervention framework and help us to begin a new RtI journey of unwavering collective commitment in honor of our children.

Dr. Mary Howard

Author

RtI from All Sides: What Every Teacher Needs to Know (Heinemann, 2009)

Moving Forward with RtI: Reading and Writing Activities for Every Instructional Setting (Heinemann, 2010)

Good to Great Teaching: Focusing on the Literacy Work that Matters (Heinemann, 2012)

Introduction

Every way teachers turn, someone is telling them that this is the *thing* that counts or this is the next *thing* we are going to do now. Or, this is the *thing* we are going to measure or this is the *thing* we used to do and are going to do again. The problem is there are a lot of *things*. There are initiatives, tools, technologies, instructional materials, assessments, and more! There are so many, it's hard to keep track. It is no wonder teachers are so tired all the time. Back in the 1980s and 1990s, there was a large research focus on teacher psychology and how to best support teachers so that they could support their students. In C.M. Clark & P.L. Peterson's article "Teachers' Thought Processes", published in the Handbook of Research on Teaching from 1986 (pp. 255-296), researchers observed elementary teachers making about 1500 decisions per day. That comes down to about 4 decisions every minute in a typical six hour school day. When we imagine the various tasks and responsibilities teachers encounter each day, I envision that number increasing over time. By training and passion, teachers are wisdom-seekers and givers, role models, restorative justice facilitators, social, academic, and emotional guides. Teachers' school days are filled with all kinds of responsibilities from nursing (it is amazing what a band-aid can solve), counseling (talking it out is what it often takes), mindfulness champion (keeping the balance makes for great minds), and acting as a compassion warrior (a hug is worth all the weight in gold), just to name a few. When thinking about all of these hats, it's not surprising that 1500 boils down to about 4 educational decisions per minute during the school day. That means that about every 15 seconds a teacher is making a decision that could (or I might argue...that should) make a difference in a child's life.

Let's live in that for a moment — four educational decisions per minute, meaning one every 15 seconds.

How do we do it? More importantly, how do we do it well? My husband might ask, *why do we do it?* If you are like me, I am sure you have asked yourself that same question. When it comes down to it, I think we show up because we got into this business to make an impact with and for kids. It is a profession where our main job is to support the overall health — emotional health, academic health, physical health — of our students. Their growth and development is not only our job, but it is impacted both in the short and long-term by the decisions we make and the support we provide. You can imagine, then, why it's so frustrating for teachers when they explain they face educational problems of practice that get in their way. Many times they feel like they do not have enough time, resources, know-how, or authority to do what is needed. In those situations, teachers do one of two things:
1. Do what has been prescribed in the past.
2. Turn their attention to limitations outside their control, like the school board policy, curriculum resources, administrative procedures, parenting, or even the students' home life.

When we do what has been prescribed in the past and/or, focus on limitations, or blame others, we reduce our problem-solving thinking to inside-the-box versus out-of-the-box thinking. Kids deserve more than that and we should hope that they expect more from us than that too. Educators face problems of practice every day. Some are light and can be solved in simple ways. Others may feel heavy and take more thought, attention, and care. Regardless, support for the kids in our care requires finding action-oriented, creative responses to our students' needs.

There is an overarching problem of practice that lingers above all of the rest — and that's the issue of *time*. I call this the *umbrella problem* because it's overarching and hovers over all aspects of our work. Rather, it's the lack of time to get everything done in a period, such as a day, a week, a month, a unit, or a year that creates the struggle. It's not that lack of time is the most important problem; it's just that it always seems to be present — no matter the circumstance. Some might argue that time is a constant challenge due to the hustle, bustle, and fast pace of our lives. For our purposes, we're going to limit our lens surrounding time to school; however, I'm not discrediting that the tug of war with time outside of the school day does not impact our work inside the school day as well.

A BRIEF HISTORICAL LOOK AT TIME IN SCHOOLS

It's a fact that the typical American school day has not changed much since the 1950s, and we just keep putting things on the plate. It doesn't matter how much schools talk about the priority of freeing up time to make room for other, more important things. The fact remains that the school day is only about 6.5-7 hours per day, Monday through Friday. There's still not enough time. That's because we always use the time we have. Maybe it's because we hang onto old things while taking on new things. Or, that we ignore the new things because we have so many old things piled up on the plate that determining what to let go of is just too much. Either way, the fact remains that letting go of something when adding something new is necessary if we want our work to be both deep and wide.

Let's take a quick look at some school attributes from the 1950s:
- A teacher's salary was about $4,000 per year.
- The decade began with segregation and ended with desegregation (due to the landmark case of *Brown v. Board of Education* in 1954).
- Slide rulers and headphones were the hip technology of the decade.
- Typewriters were used to type papers, and teachers used chalk on blackboards for teaching.
- Baseball and basketball were the only team sports at school.
- Many students walked to school, and it was not uncommon for most students to go home for lunch each day.
- The same teacher taught elementary students all subjects throughout the day.
- In many schools, students were expected to stand when addressing the teacher or answering a question.
- The length of the school year was approximately 155 days compared to 180 today.

For the most part, schools have evolved over the past seventy years. However, there are a few things that look, sound, and feel similar. Take a look!

The 1950s	Today
Charlotte's Web was a bestseller.	Charlotte's Web is still a beloved book today.
There was a concern about the amount of time school-age children were spending watching television.	There is a concern about students' use of screen time.

Class sizes were 30+.	While not indicative of all schools, class sizes can be large (28+).
The school day started around 8:30 and ended around 3:00 or 3:30. That equated to about 7 hours for a typical school day. That included time for lunch. There were approximately 6 hours dedicated to instruction.	Generally speaking, the school day starts around 8:00 and ends around 3:00 or 3:30. That equates to about 7 hours for a typical school day. That includes time for lunch. There are approximately 6 hours dedicated to instruction.

Figure 0.1 Comparison of the 1950s to Today.

It's hard to imagine that the typical American school day has remained static across all of these years. Because our education system has evolved, and we are collectively smarter, we have learned new ways of doing business. For example, we now know better practices, have better instructional materials and give better assessments that yield more favorable results. Why, then, do we have a hard time letting go of our old ways, especially when we know that doing so creates *initiative fatigue*. It's because we think of education like the clothing industry, educators say or think things like:

- *Keep it! It might be back in style in a few years.*
- *Just wait until the pendulum swings back this way again, we will be glad we did not throw it out.*
- *I think someone just made up a new name for something we have been doing for a long time. Let us just stick with what we have got.*

Education is cyclical. Things come and go and then they come back again — sometimes with a renewed definition and purpose. That's not a bad thing. What makes it have a negative connotation is when, "Initiative fatigue stems from what educators say is a new initiative touted as the savior to whatever education problem plagues you" (Stansbury, 2013, para. 2). We know that no one initiative is going to solve all problems. So, therefore, it's our job to put the new initiative or idea into context.

SOLVING THE TIME DILEMMA

Solving the time dilemma is sophisticated work. We need to put more focus on *time maximizers* versus *time gobblers*. To do so, we have to consider our ever-changing schools and students. We also need to design culturally responsive learning experiences, matching new practices to our work that honors individual students' identities while also learning about others. Then, we need to match new practices in our work with and for students. Maximizing time sounds like it might be hard, right? If it were easy, wouldn't we be doing it already? It starts with having a better understanding of five problems of practice facing educators and educational systems today. By untangling the problems that get our way of serving students, we can learn replacement practices that afford more time and opportunities to meet the students' collective and individual needs. These actions will also help us answer these guiding questions: What's our response? How can we create systems and structures to support ALL students?

THIS I BELIEVE

What does it mean to serve all students in our learning community? In other words, what does serving all students look, sound, and feel like, and how does it show up in our work?

This I Believe (What do you believe?)	I Will (How does this show up in your work?)
Every child has the right to have a teacher who is in the instructional design driver's seat, creating and implementing plans specific to the needs and wants of the students.	Teachers plan, implement, reflect, revise, plan, implement, and so on because that is their primary job.
Every teacher deserves the professional respect that is required to make instructional designs, with intentional pivots, to meet the individual and collective needs and wants of students.	Teachers do not have to go through a process, outside of the classroom, to make changes to meet the students' needs and wants. It is assumed that the teacher is always operating in that mode.
Every school should have a collaborative, inclusive mindset where *ALL students* means ALL, including the stance that EVERY child in the school has the care, insight, and collective autonomy and agency of EVERY single teacher. We have a responsibility to ALL students in our school, regardless of our role or grade level assignment.	There may be grade levels, classroom doors, and other structures that separate kids, but when we believe that ALL students in our learning community matter, it is up to the entire staff to make sure that ALL reach their goals. That means creating systems and structures that give way to teachers collaborating about all students.

Figure 0.2 This I Believe / I Will.

PROBLEMS OF PRACTICE

While not all-inclusive, I have outlined five big challenges, or *problems of practice*, that educators face consistently across the K-12 landscape. Simply put, this book is about naming these challenges specific to our current RtI models, better understanding why they exist, and putting forth ways to solve them so that we close the gap between what we want the students to be able to know, understand and do and where they are now.

Problem Of Practice #1: We Need to Break Out of the RtI Box

The RtI pyramid was created to harness support structures for all students (Fox & Hemmeter, 2009). While the intent behind it was to create a dynamic response to students' unique needs, over time, it has turned into a lock-step, machine model approach in which making decisions for students comes down to spreadsheets and flow charts instead of deep and meaningful conversations filled with multifaceted data points and dialogue.

Additionally, many policies have had negative impacts, specifically creating harmful inequities and ignoring students' identities. By placing kids in a *box* or tier, an adverse effect happens and support is either misinformed or mismatched. Instead of what should be an organic, authentic decision-making process, a boxed-in feel is created. Rethinking and redefining what we mean by *response* with and for students, coupled with when, where, why, how, and how often support will happen is a go-to for unboxing past RtI models and paving the way for a new response mindset.

Problem Of Practice #2: We Need to Honor and Increase Teacher Autonomy and Agency

Since the current RtI model boxes us in, schools have historically made decisions based on what a district-designed flowchart states as the corrective course of action rather than relying on the human capital sitting around the planning table as our greatest resource. Too often, teachers attend RtI or data meetings where their expert opinion is shortchanged by a numerical data point or a predetermined plan of action based on past practices. This process can feel like a lock-step approach, de-valuing teachers' perspectives. Overcoming this challenge requires us to not only listen to teachers, but it's also about giving them autonomy and agency to make decisions. This includes flexibility in making changes and adjustments along the way — so that they can make informed, in-the-moment moves to support their students.

Problem Of Practice #3: We Need Child Study Teams Focused on Students' Assets

Too often literacy, data, RtI, or grade-level team meetings focus on what students can't do versus what they can do. Our RtI culture feels almost as if we don't call out students' deficits, we aren't doing our job. Students, starting in kindergarten and continuing through secondary grades, have something great going for them. They have been learning since the day they were born. They bring all of that goodness with them. I am certain that a student who cannot yet independently identify and use all of the short and long vowel patterns, still has knowledge. As we utilize child study teams to create action plans, we must also prioritize equitable, educational opportunities that are culturally responsive to students' unique wants and needs. Neglecting to do so puts more students at risk. Unpacking this challenge is creating systems and structures that permit educators to start with students' assets and using those to design our responses.

Problem Of Practice #4: We Need to Increase Students' Thinking and Doing Time

My wise friend, Sam Bennett, says that, "the person who is doing the reading, writing, and thinking is the one who is doing the learning" (Bennett, 2007). I also believe that to be true. Addressing this challenge requires an analysis of how instructional time is being used. To do this, we compare the amount of teacher talk time with the amount of student thinking and doing time. If we focus on decreasing teacher talk time, students' think-time, talk-time, and work-time increases. When we hand over the learning time, students' motivation and engagement increases, creating opportunities for self-growth and success.

Problem Of Practice #5: We Need Good Instruction Because that Makes the Best Interventions

The least restrictive environment for students is most often right in their classroom, working, and learning right next to their teacher(s) and peers. That's because when instructional designs and plans are created to meet all students' wants and needs, natural interventions — a.k.a. good instruction — are intentionally built-in. It's rare for the best interventions to be delivered outside of the classroom and away from the social and academic capital that occurs in the regular classroom to yield favorable results. The goal is to design learning where the best interventions are really good, well designed, responsive instruction.

HOW IS THIS BOOK ORGANIZED?

This book is written so that readers can engage with the content from front to back, reading the chapters in order. Or, it can be read out of order, diving into the chapters that are needed at that time. At the end of Chapters 1-5, there are specific protocols that can be used to solve the *problem of practice* from that respective chapter. These protocols provide opportunities to bolster autonomy and agency across the entire organization. As you explore them, consider:

- Will teachers use these protocols independently or with a team?
- Will these protocols be used at specific times during the year or across the year?
- Will time be set aside during staff meetings or professional learning sessions (i.e. late start, early release, PD days) to utilize these protocols?
- Will you adopt these protocols OR will you adapt them to fit your purpose and audience?

Also, Chapter 6 includes a *Call to Action* advocating for our students.

There are many lenses from which to read this book. As you read, think about your role, the students you work beside, and what lens you will use to read this book. For example, a classroom teacher may enter into this work by using the tools to respond to a few students. Instructional coaches might utilize the ideas differently when leading bi-monthly data meetings. Both are important, but how you approach the protocols in this book might vary depending on your role or entry point.

READY, SET, LET'S GO!

So, are you ready to challenge yourself, and possibly your school and system to take on some common challenges facing RtI systems across the nation? Join me in this journey, sizing up five problems of practice and implementing asset-based, doable, action-oriented solutions that will change your mindset about how to support all students in your learning community. Together, we will answer the questions: What's our response? How can we create systems and structures to support ALL students?

This I Believe Protocol

Directions: Create a two-column chart (paper or digital version) naming beliefs and ways those beliefs show up in your work. You can use this protocol to design other belief statements, including each of the topics in Chapters 2-6 in this book. Also, you can name beliefs and practices with a focus on:
- Education
- Learning
- Formative Assessment
- Small-Group Instruction
- Kidwatching
- Student Work
- Motivation and Engagement
- Service and Service-Learning
- Use of Instructional Time

This I Believe Template

This I Believe (What do you believe?)	I Will (How does this show up in your work?)

Chapter 1

PROBLEM OF PRACTICE #1:
We need to break out of the RtI box.

It was a sunny, spring day and I could hear the birds chirping outside my window as the 8th grade team members trickled into our third quarter data team meeting. Computers, notebooks, coffee, and the last bites of morning breakfasts in hand, the team usually began by glancing at the data projected onto the screen. Instead, on this day, as they settled into their seats, some began to read the statement written on the whiteboard:

> Maybe it's time to break out of the RtI box.

Dan, 8th grade ELA teacher, read the words and shoved back his chair from the table and let out a big moan of disgust.

"Come on!", he said. "You mean the state is changing the RtI graphic again?"

Jaz immediately chimed in, "What? Where did you hear that? They can't do that, didn't they just do that last year?"

Kari, special educator extraordinaire, opened up her computer and quickly searched the state website for updates.

Stacey, the bright-eyed, twenty-one-year-old, student-teacher said, "What

RtI box? Isn't it a pyramid? A right-side up pyramid or sometimes a flipped, upside-down pyramid?"

Then, Evelyn, the twenty-nine-year veteran and *team Matriarch* chimed in and said, "No, I don't think the state is changing the graphic, I think Julie is asking *US* that question."

Let's pause for a moment. Have you ever been a part of a meeting that sounded like that? If you have, you get it. You can probably feel the aggravation Dan was feeling when he thought things were changing again or, Jaz's disbelief in hearing some unwanted news. You may even know a teacher like Kari who needs to get clarity on the situation before reacting. My hope is we all know and can relate to the eager-to-learn student-teacher and Evelyn types because let's face it, we need them on our teams. The new teachers keep us on our toes. The wise, veteran voices keep us grounded, helping us find balance. They help us see things for what they are because they have been around to see the pendulum swing back and forth — most likely more than once.

Right about now Melissa walked in and said, "Sorry, I am late." She slowed her pace and questioned, "Are we having our RtI data meeting right now?"

You see, Melissa was confused. That's because she was about four minutes late to our meeting and she knows, from past experiences, that this meeting type is typically very structured.

There is about 1 minute to exchange pleasantries, then onto the spreadsheet data where we talk about students' present levels, then a discussion about who will serve which students over the next three to six weeks, then a quick conversation about strategies that could be used (with an occasional pause to research something on Intervention Central, the site that had been deemed holy and vetted for listing approved *research-based interventions*), and then onto the next student and so on.

All of these rituals were well-intentioned. Reading about it sounds a little like the teachers were robotic and didn't care about kids. That's not the case at all. The reason I wrote the question on the whiteboard and posed it to this group specifically was because of their inquiry and dedication to the students in their care.

There is so much more to share about that 8th grade data team, but first, let's pause and shift our focus to how this process came to be to begin with — not only for this team but for districts, schools, teams, and teachers across the nation.

NAMING THE PROBLEM

Problem Of Practice #1: We need to break out of the RtI box.

According to the RtI Action Network, "The accountability movement in the United States (led primarily by the No Child Left Behind Act) was forcing schools to pay much more attention to the achievement of all of their students." The RtI Movement, created to address the concerns surrounding methods and practices for supporting adequate student growth, has been an ongoing topic of study for nearly three decades. While so many of the RtI Movement's actions and decision-making process are in direct conflict with my beliefs about how we can best support the students we serve, we agree on one very important aspect which is: **It is the educational system's job to provide learning opportunities to meet the needs of ALL students.**

I think the founders of the RtI Movement might even get behind my beliefs about our responsibility to students. Here's my thinking:

BELIEFS ABOUT OUR RESPONSIBILITY TO STUDENTS

I believe it is ALL students' free and public education right to expect the community, district, school, grade-level band, team, and teachers to:
- Figure out what ALL students know, understand, and can do.
- Align curriculum, instructional materials, learning opportunities to match ALL students' individual and collective needs.
- Meet the needs of ALL students — figuring out students' strengths and areas where they need a lift.
- Measure what matters.

Figure 1.1 Beliefs About Our Responsibility to Students.

The interesting part is I talk about this RtI Movement as if it's a group of people who created a committee who meet once a month to govern our educational systems and guide our decision-making processes. That's because, when you are in schools trying to live out mandates that have been put in place, based on legislation that has been passed and then interpreted in different ways, it feels like a force to be reckoned with. But, here's the thing. There isn't a committee filled with people who meet once a month and pass down judgments. That simply does not exist. Instead, what has happened is simply a reaction to the state of education at the time coupled with another reaction, and then another reaction, and another. That has led to many policies that have had impacts, often negative, specifically creating harmful inequities. Let's take a closer look.

The goal of the No Child Left Behind Act of 2001(NCLB in effect from 2001-2015) was to create equity and access for disadvantaged, minority students and those who are faced with poverty, those receiving special education services, and those who speak limited or no English.

Good idea, right?

Not really. Testing became the main information source determining if students were reaching success. Words like *proficient* and *Adequate Yearly Progress* (AYP), became a thing because of this act. With teacher accountability systems on steroids, teaching to the test became more of the norm. Labeling students using deficit terms, based on test scores, became the new normal. In the article, Why the Academic Achievement Gap is a Racist Idea, Dr. Ibram X. Kendi (2016) explains:

> Americans have been led to believe that intelligence is like body weight, and the different intellectual levels of different people can be measured on a single, standardized weight scale. Our faith in standardized tests causes us to believe that the racial gap in test scores means something is wrong with the Black test takers—and not the tests.

Then, Response to Intervention and IDEA in 2004 established a process to support students who were struggling.

Good idea, right?

Not really. This required the use of "scientific, research-based interventions" in general education, the measurement of a child's response to these interventions, and the use of the RtI data to inform instruction. This created a rub because it was difficult to get consensus around the definition and use of "scientific, research-based interventions." In Gholdy Muhammad's (2019)

Cultivating Genius: An Equity Framework for Culturally and *Historically Responsive Literacy*, she talks about teachers intentionally incorporating learning standards around students' identity through the lessons and units they create. In Muhammad's (2020) *Rethinking What Matters: Incorporating Anti-Racism into Teaching*, the author suggests, "moving beyond skills and connecting learning to students' lives and identities". Muhammad urges our response, through our planning, to include students knowing who they are, with a strong sense of self to help create confidence and truth around the history of all people. If we follow that lead, that would mean that our actions would be in response to students, their wants, needs, and their identities, rather than "scientific, research-based interventions" which are based on tested skills, rather than student identities.

With innovation and technology tools on the rise, coupled with new standards, new ways were created of testing both students and teachers through accountability systems. This time it brought about a dichotomous, often inequitable, approach to decision-making, resulting in the RtI triangle boxing us in.

HOW THE RtI TRIANGLE HAS BOXED US IN

Whether it is the typical RtI pyramid or the upside-down pyramid or the three-tiered cone or the triple building block representation, organizations across the globe have worked to interpret, design, and use a scaffolded structure for student support commonly referred to as tiered interventions. The problem with all of them is simple: It puts a label on kids and boxes them in. In serious ways, it boxes us all in. By placing a child into a tier of support, a statement is made. It says, "this is who you are and this is what we are going to do about it." It certainly does not take into account students' lives, backgrounds, and identities. I don't know about you, but the teachers I have worked with across the years have explained that they feel THEY need a Tier 3 support for supporting students in Tier 3. They laugh, but they're not really joking around. Here's another thing. The tiered intervention has lots of rules, and a lot of problems, around it. In Austin Channing Brown's podcast, she refers to a conversation she had with Kelly Hurst who nudges us to ask these two important questions: "Who does this policy help? Who does this policy harm?" (Channing-Brown, 2020). Let's keep these questions in mind as we unpack typical RtI rules and the problems those rules create.

Rules	Problems
• Only a certain number of kids should be in each tier at one time.	• Living in numbers versus real-time needs is a dangerous game that puts students and schools at risk.
• The frequency, intensity, and duration of the intervention depend more on the tier than it does on the student.	• This makes serving students so complicated. If we spend too much time analyzing our analysis of support, we will miss the good stuff of actually helping students.
• A student is always in Tier 1 because that is the classroom level work. But, if they are in another Tier, their work might be different than that in Tier 1.	• This creates a lack of clarity and continuity.
• Many times, RtI is the path for students to obtain a Special Education designation.	• Overuse and overidentification of Special Education designations often create academic, social, and economic disparities, even with the best intentions.

Figure 1.2 Rules / Problems.

One way to combat the problems associated with the *rules* of RtI, is to unpack how some of the *rules* were established at the onset and consider ways to navigate or eliminate the challenges.

FREQUENCY, INTENSITY, DURATION

Guideposts are important. They give us a frame of reference for how success has been reached in the past so that we may also find success. We find guideposts in the directions when baking a new recipe, when looking at the diagram showing how to install a new ink cartridge in the printer, and which way to turn when entering the parking lot. We live within guideposts all of the time, whether we realize it or not.

The RtI Movement needed some guideposts — a way of sorting out all of the details that were coming to the surface. Since supporting students is important business, school districts, schools and teacher teams were in search of answers to questions such as:

- What does support look like? How much is enough? What is too little?
- How often should I meet with students? For how long?

As you can imagine, lots of people had lots of different opinions. There were some terms with agreed-upon definitions that were helpful.

FREQUENCY: How often instruction occurs or repeats across a given time (Ex. Every other day)

INTENSITY: The amount of energy put into the instruction (Ex. Group size, proximity, resource selection)

DURATION: The amount of time for instruction (Ex. 45 minutes)

These three terms can create havoc unless they are used as a system. The pivotal word in this trio is INTENSITY because it is the action, in my opinion, that is the change-maker. Here is an example:

I had the pleasure of supporting Lori, a 6th grade math teacher and her team. By design, we created small groups that met three times each week. During the math block, we worked together in the classroom alongside small groups. We noticed Isaac and Eli having trouble using the data to construct a coordinate plane. During an after school co-planning session, we discussed what was working, what wasn't working, and why the boys may be experiencing confusion. Even though we created a theory about the potential confusion, we decided the only way we will know is to get up close to the conversation. As a result, we decided to listen in closely to the small group work, increasing our intensity through proximity, to get a better understanding of the boys' knowledge. After that, we met and brainstormed different learning opportunities for Isaac and Eli such as:
- Change or adjust small group learning opportunities for Isaac and Eli
- Change small group sizes to match the needs of the class
- Extend or shorten each small group learning opportunity experience
- Meet with students one-to-one
- Keep things the way they are because they are working

As I co-design support options with teachers and teams, I like to use frequency, intensity, and duration as one way to think about the many different, dynamic ways there are to create support systems and routines for students. One way to do this is to create a Menu of Support Options.

MENU OF SUPPORT OPTIONS

If we do not want to live in a machine model where all of our options are already pre-determined for us, then we must be ready to put the puzzle together during data team meetings. Take a look at Figure 1.3. Here I outline an example of how the typical interpretation of RtI has played out in our educational systems. As you explore the ideas, imagine a student you know well. Think about his/her assets and areas where he/she needs a lift. Then, imagine where you'd place him/her on Figure 1.3 and the support that might follow. Do you think he/she will reach success? Why or why not?

What	Tier 1	Tier 2	Tier 3	Tier 4
Frequency/ Length of Intervention Lessons/ Sessions	Classroom Instruction & Intervention	2-3 times per week	Daily or 4-5 times per week	Special Education
Amount of Time per Lesson/ Session		30-45 minutes	45-60 minutes	
Duration of Intervention Cycle		6-8 Weeks	6-8 weeks depending on the instructional program	
Size of Instructional Group		4-6 students	1:1, 1:2 or 1:3	
Who Typically Delivers the Intervention?	Classroom Teacher	Specialist or Special Education Teacher	Specialist or Special Education Teacher	
Where is the Intervention Delivered?	Classroom	Specialist or Special Education Teacher's Classroom	Specialist or Special Education Teacher's Classroom	Special Education Teacher's Classroom

*Specialist = Professionals with Specialized Certificates

Figure 1.3 Typical RtI Support Structure.

Now, look at Figure 1.4 and take a moment to note the slight differences between the semantics used compared to Figure 1.3. For each reference, the differences have been noted in bold. Keeping that same student in mind, with a focus on assets and areas needing a lift, think about where you'd place him/her on Figure 1.4 and the support that might follow.

Problem of Practice #1

What	Tier 1	Tier 2	Tier 3	Tier 4
Frequency/ Length of **Instruction** Lessons/ Sessions	Classroom Instruction & Intervention	2-3 times per week	Daily or 4-5 times per week	Special Education
Amount of Time per Lesson/ Session		30-45 minutes	45-60 minutes	
Duration of **Instruction** Cycle		6-8 Weeks	6-8 weeks depending on the instructional program	
Size of Instructional Group		**Depending on students' wants and needs** **Teacher to Student 1:1, 1:2 or 1:3** **Student to Student Groups of 2-6**		
Who Typically Delivers the **Instruction**?	Classroom Teacher	**Classroom Teacher**, Specialist or Special Education Teacher	**Classroom Teacher**, Specialist or Special Education Teacher	
Where is the **Instruction** Delivered?	Classroom	**Classroom <u>and</u>** Specialist or Special Education Teacher's Classroom	**Classroom <u>and</u>** Specialist or Special Education Teacher's Classroom	**Classroom Teacher <u>and</u>** Special Education Teacher's Classroom

*Specialist = Professionals with Specialized Certificates

Figure 1.4 Asset-Based, Least Restrictive Support Structure.

Did your thinking about ways to create support structures for this student change? Do you think he/she will reach success? Why or why not?

REOPENING OLD WOUNDS

Many of the changes that RtI created put educators on edge. In some cases, it meant groups of people putting up their *fighting gloves* and heading to their corners. Put another way, this time shined a light on sticking with your *camp*. Depending on how long you've been an educator, you might ask: Who were these camps? Where are their head offices located? Who leads them and how do they get funding? Have these camps been around for a long time? Do these camps still exist? These camps, dating back to the 40+ years, maybe even longer, represent the ongoing battle between groups such as:

- Phonics versus whole language
- Direct instruction versus inquiry-based learning
- The science of reading versus the art and science of teaching reading
- Curriculum-based measurements versus developmental assessments
- Ability grouping versus flexible grouping
- State testing versus no state testing
- Retention versus no retention

Opposites have a tough time finding a common ground, making it difficult to see beyond what is in your *corner*. During this time, educators felt as though they were being judged under the microscope, often operating out of fear and criticism versus support, which only widened the divide.

OVERPRODUCTION OF EDUCATIONAL PRODUCTS

In addition to reopening old wounds and with the distinct possibility of making new ones, interested groups, organizations, consortiums, professional developers, for-profit companies designing and selling instructional materials, and online assessment systems created solutions to the current educational landscape. Many were sold as *one-stop solutions meeting all your needs* and often filled with empty or understudied promises. In turn, when this *full-proof* product didn't work, it was perceived by some that it must be either the teacher or the student that was causing the struggle, not the product. Exhausting, right? Well, it was exhausting because what this created was far worse than a flooded market filled with products. The real issue is that it caused teachers to not trust themselves, and in some cases, it created a lack of trust between district leaders, teachers, and families. When the products did not work, leadership sometimes blamed the teachers. The teachers blamed the products or the kids. The parents/caregivers blamed the schools and, in turn, the teachers.

While I am talking about these issues as if they are in the past, you may concur that the impacts from the RtI Movement are still hanging on today. Let's turn now to naming beliefs and applying some solution-oriented responses.

THIS I BELIEVE

This I Believe (What do you believe?)	**I Will** (How does this show up in your work?)
The community, district, school, grade-level band, team, and teachers have a responsibility to figure out what ALL students know, understand, and can do.	Use developmental and holistic assessments to assess students' knowledge, skills, and understandings to create a responsive and differentiated focus for instruction.
It is our job to align curriculum, instructional materials, learning opportunities to match ALL students' individual and collective needs.	Collaboratively planning units of study/learning progressions to include materials and learning experiences that match all student needs.
Students are depending on us to figure out their strengths and areas where they need a lift.	Design learning that will extend students' strengths and support areas where they need a lift.
We must measure what matters.	Use formative assessment to guide planning across the unit of study and use end demonstrations of learning to measure student growth.

Figure 1.5 This I Believe / I Will.

WHAT CAN WE DO ABOUT IT?

There is an old Shel Silverstein poem that references these lines:

> "When the light turns green, you go. When the light turns red, you stop. But what do you do when the light turns blue with orange and lavender spots?"

If you know Shel Silverstein, known for children's poetry and by some for his career as a song lyric writer and cartoonist, his unique style invites readers to interpret his work and take away from it what they need and want. In this spirit, I lean on the lines from Silverstein's (1981), *A Light in the Attic*, because it encourages us to live and learn and act in a not-so-exact sort of way. It permits us to not live in the black and white, but instead the gray. It may sound scary or haphazard or unprepared, but what I believe we need to plan for are the in-between parts — learning to make decisions with and for students when the "light turns blue with orange spots". Doing so might yield asset-based, action-oriented solutions founded on beliefs about ALL students' free and public educational rights. If we want this to really happen we will have to ensure a few things:

1. If we want to know what ALL students know, understand, and can do, we will have to drop the levels and labels. That's because when we box students into a level or label, they size themselves up (and so do we), putting a box around what success already looks like.
2. If we want to align curriculum, instructional materials, and learning opportunities to match ALL students' individual and collective needs, we will have to be critical connoisseurs of marketed materials. That means teacher teams reviewing and vetting curriculum, instruction, and assessment products with a laser focus on diverse and culturally responsive materials. Also, providing teacher teams the autonomy and agency to co-create products to meet the needs of their learning community should be a high priority.
3. If we want to meet the needs of ALL students, then using in-real-time, on-the-spot assessment data — from both teachers and students — is essential. That means that easy-to-use, inexpensive, responsive, natural tools need to be used to take stock of students' strengths and areas needing a lift.
4. If we want to help students grow into productive, learn-at-your-fingertips, impact the world in front of you kind of adults, we have to give them a dress rehearsal to do those same sophisticated and compelling things now. We will have to plan learning opportunities with that mindset and then make sure that the ways we measure what we say matters mimics real-world experiences versus stand-alone measures.

DATA MODELS ARE ONLY AS GOOD AS OUR ASSUMPTIONS

Data is a funny thing. First of all, the word *data* is not singular, it is plural. The singular of data is datum. So often, we say the "data is" when we mean "data are". This matters because it naturally fits with prioritizing multiple data points, of varying types, when we are talking about students' assets and areas needing a lift. Too often, data teams come around the table and what is displayed on the screen is a number, let's say from a Curriculum-Based Measure (CBM). That datum is color-coded (red for a *red flag*, orange for on the *watch list*, green for *meets expectation*) and there is an immediate response. We make assumptions about that student based on that information. I am not suggesting that all school data team meetings stop there. What I am saying is that something happens to us naturally as soon as we see that datum color-coded. We put that student, whether we want to or not, into a box or category. It is natural for people to look for patterns and naturally group things. It is actually how we make sense of the world around us. The problem is, once that CBM is mixed together with other datum, such as the latest developmental assessment, teacher observations, and student work samples, it turns into DATA. When we add variables — or new data — models change and our response might need to change as well. If we continue down the same path without pausing to reflect on the new data model, we risk making too many assumptions. This very idea is what makes data so interesting and so irritating. If we believe in the data we are collecting and sizing up, then data meetings have to be fluid and flexible. Our actions and reactions should be an on-going response to academic, social-emotional, and physical triangulation of the data because our models are only as good as our assumptions about the data in that given moment. That is why it is our responsibility to always ask: What's our response?

REMEMBER THE 8TH GRADE TEAM?

If you recall, the 8th grade team entered a data team meeting where I posed the question:

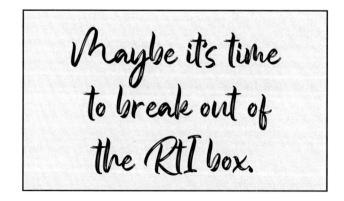

After they settled and realized that the state or district hadn't changed things up and that Evelyn was right, I just wanted to pose the question to launch a discussion, we settled into what would become months and months of great work. Before we had a chance to name whether or not it was time to break out of the RtI box, we first had to take stock of our current reality. To do this, I asked for a safe and free-flowing conversation around this stem.

> We are _____ rich and _____ poor.
> (Fill in the blanks)

Here is their first attempt at what they said:

We are data rich, insight poor.
We are resource rich, selection poor.
We are vision rich, operational poor.
We are assessment rich, response poor.
We are opportunity rich, time poor.

This initial snapshot gave us entry points into what would become a really important short and long term conversation, not only with the 8th grade team but with all middle school staff in the district. We asked ourselves if we are data rich and insight poor:
- What makes us data rich?
- What is getting in our way and making us insight poor?
- What steps do we take to create a data rich, insight rich environment?
- How will we know we have achieved a data rich, insight rich environment?

We also asked ourselves if we are vision rich and operational poor:
- What is our vision and why would we label it vision rich?
- What is getting in our way and making us operational poor?
- What steps do we take to create a vision rich, operational rich environment?
- How will we know we have achieved a vision rich, operational rich environment?

It's amazing what putting really smart, dedicated teachers together to talk about two question stems can do to help shift a system. The 8th grade team, all of them including Stacey who joined the team the following fall as the newest 8th grade team member, worked for the next two years. They used some of the tools and protocols included in this chapter and this book to break out of the RtI box and co-create their response to supporting ALL students' collective and individual needs.

Defining Frequency, Duration, Intensity Protocol

Directions: Invite participants to come together to create an Asset-Based, Least Restrictive Support Structure by defining the frequency, duration, and intensity of support.

Materials: Copy of *Asset-Based, Least Restrictive Support Structure* planning grid and/or a blank copy of the grid (paper or digital version)

Step 1: Ask the question: What's our response? How do we support and serve students in our care?

Step 2: Using the example called *Asset-Based, Least Restrictive Support Structure*, discuss the benefits and shortfalls of this plan.

Step 3: Determine whether you will adopt or adapt the example provided and create a draft plan.
- Will you change or adjust any language?
- Will you add or delete any sections?

Step 4: Decide what other stakeholders should preview the draft and provide feedback.
- Teachers?
- Committee?
- Advisory Board?

Step 5: Make changes to the draft based on feedback. Create a final version. Share it with stakeholders.

Step 6: Create a timeline for when this group will come back together to reflect and/or make any needed adjustments.

PROTOCOL

Asset-Based, Least Restrictive Support Structure Example

What	Tier 1	Tier 2	Tier 3	Tier 4
Frequency/ Length of Instruction Lessons/ Sessions	Classroom Instruction & Intervention	2-3 times per week	Daily or 4-5 times per week	Special Education
Amount of Time per Lesson/ Session		30-45 minutes	45-60 minutes	
Duration of Instruction Cycle		6-8 Weeks	6-8 weeks depending on the instructional program	
Size of Instructional Group		\multicolumn{2}{l}{Depending on students' wants and needs. Teacher to Student 1:1, 1:2 or 1:3. Student to Student Groups of 2-6}	
Who Typically Delivers the Instruction?	Classroom Teacher	Classroom Teacher, Specialist or Special Education Teacher	Classroom Teacher, Specialist or Special Education Teacher	Classroom Teacher and Special Education Teacher
Where is the Instruction Delivered?	Classroom	Classroom and Specialist or Special Education Teacher's Classroom	Classroom and Specialist or Special Education Teacher's Classroom	Classroom and Special Education Teacher's Classroom

*Specialist = Professionals with Specialized Certificates

Asset-Based, Least Restrictive Support Structure Template (Blank)

What	Tier 1	Tier 2	Tier 3	Tier 4
Frequency/ Length				
Amount of Time				
Duration				
Size of Instructional Group				
Who				
Where				

PROTOCOL

Creating A Menu Of Support Protocol

Directions: Invite participants to come together to create a Menu of Support. Explain that this dynamic document, known as the "Menu", will become a storage warehouse for ideas related to different ways teachers, teacher teams, and families/caregivers can support students. Select one of the *Menu of Support Planning* Templates and/or use a blank version of the grid (paper or digital version) to begin planning student support options.

Step 1: Decide who you are planning support for: Whole class, a small group, or individual students.

Step 2: Choose a category and ask: How do we create responsive support for students?

Whole Class	Small Group	Individual Students
• What does the whole class need?	• What does the small group need?	• What does the student need?
• Who will teach/support it?	• Who will teach/support it?	• Who will teach/support it?
• When will it be taught/supported?	• When will it be taught/supported?	• When will it be taught/supported?
• Where will it be taught/supported?	• Where will it be taught/supported?	• Where will it be taught/supported?
• Why is this needed?	• Why is this needed?	• Why is this needed?
• How will it be taught/supported?	• How will it be taught/supported?	• How will it be taught/supported?
• How long will it be taught/supported?	• How long will it be taught/supported?	• How long will it be taught/supported?
• How will we know it worked or did not work?	• How will we know it worked or did not work?	• How will we know it worked or did not work?

Step 3: Use a template to collect responses to the questions posed.

Step 4: Decide when the group will come back together to reflect. Consider asking:
- When should we come back together and reflect on this process and the Menu of Support we have created?
- What evidence of impact should we be prepared to share with others?

Add/change the list below to fit the needs and ideas of participants:
- ○ Student work samples (in process work or final products)
- ○ Teacher observations / notes
- ○ Numerical data accompanied by anecdotal notes or work samples
- ○ Student testimonials or reflections

PROTOCOL

Menu of Support Planning Template #1 (Blank)

Name _____

Team Members _____

Date _____

WHO (student)	WHAT (actions)	WHEN	WHERE	WHY	HOW	FOR HOW LONG

Menu of Support Planning Template #2 (Blank)

Name _____

Team Members _____

Date _____

What	Our Actions (who, what, when, where, why, how, how often)	Our Reflections (What did we learn after putting our actions into action?)	Our Wonderings (What are we wondering now?)

Menu of Support Planning Template #3 (Literacy)

Name _____

Team Members _____

Date _____

What	Our Actions (who, what, when, where, why, how, how often)	Our Reflections (What did we learn after putting our actions into action?)	Our Wonderings (What are we wondering now?)
What can students read during independent reading, small group work, and at home?			
What real-world reading and writing projects can students create in response to their thinking and new understandings?			

Menu of Support Planning Template #4 (Math)

Name _____

Team Members _____

Date _____

What	Our Actions (who, what, when, where, why, how, how often)	Our Reflections (What did we learn after putting our actions into action?)	Our Wonderings (What are we wondering now?)
What can students solve/figure out during independent math time, small group work, and at home?			
What real-world math projects can students create in response to their thinking and new understandings?			

PROTOCOL

Menu of Support Planning Template #5 (By Week)

Student(s):

	Week 1	Week 2	Week 3	Week 4
Structure Whole Group Small Group 1:1				
Academic Content				
Other Supports				

Menu of Support Planning Template #6 (By Month)

Student(s):

	September	**October-December**	**January-March**	**April-June**
Structure Whole Group Small Group 1:1				
Academic Content				
Other Supports				

Problem of Practice #1

Sizing Up Our "Wealth" Protocol

Directions: Invite participants to come together and size up our collective wealth.

Say: Schools are living, breathing, dynamic environments that have the ability, and often the challenge, to pivot and change regularly. Taking a moment to pause and size up our collective wealth helps us reflect on the past, take stock of the present, and plan for the future.

Step 1: Individually or collaboratively, fill in the missing parts using this stem. Add as many ideas as you would like. You can think about:
- The system as a whole (education in general or your respective district)
- The community as a whole (communities in general or your respective community)
- The school as a whole (schools in general or your respective school)
- The classroom as a whole (classrooms in general or your respective classroom)
- The adult learner as a whole (adults in general or your respective school or team)
- The student learner as a whole (the K-12 student in general or students in your school or team)

> We are _____ rich and _____ poor.
> (Fill in the blanks)

Note of Caution: Do not fall into the trap of playing the blame game. For example, do not begin naming people or places because it will take you down a deficit, unprofessional path. Keep it specific enough to get the idea moving and generic enough to stay in the asset-based, collegial mindset.

Step 2: Invite participants to share out. Consider creating a shared space for these ideas to be stored so that they can be referenced later.

Step 3: Ask participants: Are there any statements you have listed that you believe needs attention and action? If so, what are they? Participants can mark the high priority statements with a star.

For example, if someone shares that the grade level is "vision rich, but math manipulative poor" and there is consensus around that being a priority, together you could create a plan for how to change that current reality.

Step 4: Ask participants: Look at your high priority statements. What action steps can we create to make changes? Using the example above, what actions can we take to become "vision rich and math manipulative rich"?

Step 5: Give participants time to create or co-create an action-oriented plan.

Step 6: Once plans have been put into action, create opportunities for participants to share celebrations and next steps.

PROTOCOL

Teacher Self-Reflection Protocol:
Breaking Out Of The RtI Box

Directions: The support structures we provide to students are multi-faceted. Take time to self-reflect using the questions as a guide.

Self-Reflection: Breaking Out of the RtI Box

Question	Self-Assessment					What do you need next? What are your next steps?
I/we have created an asset-based, least restrictive support structure to meet the needs of ALL learners.	Seldom 1	2	Some of the time 3	4	Most of the time 5	
I/we have created a Menu of Support to meet the needs of ALL learners.	Seldom 1	2	Some of the time 3	4	Most of the time 5	

What's Our Response?

What needs to happen to ensure that we are not boxed in and that we are creating support that is asset-based and prioritizes the least restrictive environment for ALL students? List steps or bullet points to describe your perspective.

Asset-Based, Least Restrictive Environment Support

Problem of Practice #1

Chapter 2

PROBLEM OF PRACTICE #2:
We need to honor and increase teacher autonomy and agency.

When teachers share that they often know what to do when their students need support, but that they do not have the authority to make those decisions, it makes me pause and wonder. The questions that bubble to the surface from this type of statement are numerous. I cannot think about this without bringing my 28+ years of experience as an educator into play. That's because for the first ten years, or more, of my teaching career if I even muttered that type of stance, it would have created red flags around my intentions and know-how in teaching my students. Back in the early 1990s, we did not question our authority as classroom teachers to make instructional decisions that were in the best interest of our students. Instead, we were empowered to find and use what was needed to help students grow. In those days, some unwritten rules were assumed when you stepped into the teacher role. Some of those included:

- You did not wait for a data team meeting to make a plan of action for a student. You made the plan, executed it, documented it, and reached out for assistance if you needed colleagues to help you brainstorm different solutions.
- You did not wait for someone to give you access to data, current or past. You used on-the-spot assessments to determine students' strengths and areas of need. You also went to the students' cumulative file, where many past assessments were housed, and used all of that data to build a narrative about students. Also, if you needed to better understand a student's history, you met with previous teachers and communicated with parents, either formally or informally. In most cases, you were taught to log all of your thinking and steps through anecdotal notes in the binder where you kept all of the important information about the students in your care.

- You did not try an intervention for three weeks, meet about your findings with a team, and then create a new plan for the next three weeks and so on. Instead, you (the classroom teacher) made plans each day, which included adjustments for specific children, and you made instructional decisions every week or so (sometimes every few days) depending on the child's response. Timing of support was not based on a protocol, but rather your interactions with students.
- You did not push students out of the classroom for support. Students remained in the classroom, except for extreme cases.
- You did not refer students to a process that would lead to special education. That was reserved for students with severe learning disabilities.
- You did not spend time talking about how selected programs, instructional materials, and interventions that a team designed are not working. If you knew that something would work, you tried it. If it was not working, it was up to you to make a change and, more importantly, seek the advice and guidance of colleagues if learning for a student had stalled.

Were those days mess-free? No, of course not. At times, teachers felt isolated and left to their own problem-solving devices. Instead of research-based strategies, there was more of a *grab bag* strategy approach. Sometimes those strategies worked, other times not. We relied on developmental assessments for reading and math, which was helpful, but we were less sophisticated and strategic because we did not know as much then about how to design formative assessments focused on what students knew, understood, and could do which made figuring out next steps sometimes difficult. However, what those days did create was a heightened sense of professionalism — a *we've got this* mindset — that is often absent today. Being a teacher felt a lot like being a physician. It felt like you were a trusted advisor of the overarching educational health and well-being of each student. We took pride in the decisions we made. We celebrated the successes, and we lost sleep over the challenges we could not quite unravel. The constant in the work was getting up every day to help each child succeed. Teachers were trusted researchers, working to solve the challenges, misconceptions, and misunderstandings in the students right in front of them. Growth for all students was an implied imperative. Since our research included living, breathing, dynamic, sophisticated students each day, getting them involved as partners in this work made complete sense. Conferring regularly, co-hosting student-led conferences, and on-going family share nights became the norm. It was a messy, busy time. It was a beautiful, organic, and authentic time too.

NAMING THE PROBLEM

Problem Of Practice #2: We Need to Honor and Increase Teacher Autonomy and Agency.

Before we dig into this problem of practice, let's focus on some working definitions of two specific terms.

WHAT ARE AUTONOMY AND AGENCY?

Autonomy and agency can mean different things to different people, not to mention they are used differently in other areas such as business and agriculture. For our purposes, I am using the following working definitions as a basis.

AUTONOMY: Having the capacity to act, to self-govern, to make decisions on your own. Having a feeling of empowerment and independence.

AGENCY: Having the will to take action and be an agent of change.

In some ways, you can see how these terms might be used synonymously. For me, the difference is slight but significant. Autonomy is about an internal mindset. Agency is about taking action.

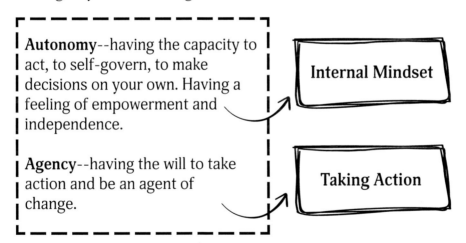

Teachers believing that they have both and can or should use both in their work is essential. I'm reminded of some wise advice from Dr. Mary Howard. *In Good to Great Teaching: Focusing on the Literacy Work that Matters* (2012), she says, "There are many things you can't control, but you can control the quality of your work in the confines of your classroom" (p. 25). I believe that to my core. A first step in honoring and increasing teacher autonomy and agency, is to declare our beliefs.

THIS I BELIEVE

This I Believe (What do you believe?)	I Will (How does this show up in your work?)
Every child has the right to have a teacher who is in the instructional design driver's seat, creating and implementing plans specific to the needs and wants of the students.	Teachers plan, implement, reflect, revise, plan, implement, and so on because that is their #1 job.
Every teacher deserves the professional respect that is required to make instructional designs, with intentional pivots, to meet the individual and collective needs and wants of students.	Teachers do not have to go through a process, outside of the classroom, to make changes to meet students' needs and wants. It is assumed that the teacher is always operating in that mode.
Every school should have a collaborative, inclusive mindset where *ALL students* means ALL. This includes the stance that EVERY child in the school has the care, insight, and collective autonomy and agency of EVERY single teacher.	There may be grade levels, classroom doors, and other structures that separate kids, but when we believe that ALL students in our learning community matter, it is up to the entire staff to make sure that ALL reach their goals. That means creating systems and structures that give way to teachers collaborating about all students.

Figure 2.1 This I Believe / I Will.

AREAS OF AUTONOMY AND AGENCY

As I work with teams across the country composed of key district stakeholders such as administrators, teachers, and support staff, I ask: *In general, when, where, how, and how often do teachers have voice and choice (autonomy) and put it into action (agency)?* What surfaces is that there are areas that teachers have autonomy and agency and areas where autonomy and agency are absent or limited. Here is a pattern that emerged from their responses:

Voice & Choice	Absence of OR Limited Voice & Choice
• Classroom set-up & design • Classroom management systems, routines, and rituals • Building trusting relationships with students, families, and colleagues • Homework • How to use time that has been allocated for learning (example: how the time during the ELA block is allocated) • Communication/outreach with families • Textbook (when it is listed as a resource vs. a page-by-page, day-by-day manuscript) • Delivery of instruction, assessment, and intervention • Use of technology & school library/media center resources (frequency and duration) • Classroom library design • Unit/Learning Progression/Lesson Plan Template	• State standards • State testing • Assessment systems purchased by the district • Required district assessments • District benchmarks • Staff meeting, data team meeting, PLC/team meeting attendance • Horizontal/Vertical Articulation Meeting attendance • District pacing guides/curricular calendars (if applicable)

Figure 2.2. Voice & Choice vs. Absence of OR Limited Voice & Choice.

I get excited when I see a list like this because I see positive opportunities and entry points for our work in schools. Instead of focusing on the things we can't control, I like to focus on the areas where we do have some control. I would rather teachers have voice and choice over classroom design, building relationships with students, and use of instructional time compared to state testing. Don't get me wrong, anyone who knows me can attest to my dislike of state tests, but if I had to choose I would choose the former over the latter any day!

The list on the right in Figure 2.2 often creates an absence or limited voice and choice for educators and while those things govern us, they don't keep us from creating dynamic, solution-oriented responses. As educators, when we feel a little bit stuck, we have to remind ourselves about the many things we have in our locus of control that have a direct impact on students.

Let's take some time to unpack a similar list concerning a RtI process. The question I pose is: *Concerning your current RtI model or process, when, where, how, and how often do teachers have voice and choice (autonomy) and put it into action (agency)?* Here is a pattern that has emerged from their responses:

Voice & Choice	Absence of OR Limited Voice & Choice
• Referring students to the data team • Giving off-cycle benchmark assessments (if provided by district) • Process by which anecdotal notes/records are recorded	• Data meeting schedule and attendance • Meeting guest list (inviting stakeholders) • Documentation forms • State testing • Assessment systems purchased by the district • Required district assessments • District benchmarks • District pacing guides/curricular calendars (if applicable)

Figure 2.3 Voice & Choice vs. Absence of OR Limited Voice & Choice in RtI.

The list on the right in Figure 2.3, where there is a perception of an absence of or limited voice and choice, did not surprise me. It's natural for teachers to feel like they have limited voice in meeting schedules, documentation forms, and district assessments. However, what did surprise me was the list on the left in Figure 2.3. When nudged to share more details, teachers mentioned the additional ideas highlighted in bold in Figure 2.4.

Voice & Choice	Absence of OR Limited Voice & Choice
• Referring students to the data team • Giving off-cycle benchmark assessments (if provided by district) • Process by which anecdotal notes/records are recorded • **Adjusting Tier 1 instruction, daily or weekly** • **Increasing the frequency, duration, and intensity when meeting with students** • **Creating flexible small group learning opportunities to meet students' collective and individual needs** • **Using students' assets to create a focus for instruction** • **Creating ongoing, authentic formative assessments to inform instruction and guide next steps** • **Using student work products to inform instruction and guide next steps** • **Classroom set-up & design to meet students' needs** • **How to use time that has been allocated for learning (example: how the time during the ELA block is allocated)** • **Communication/collaboration with families** • **Use of technology, school library/media center resources, manipulatives, and tools**	• Data meeting schedule and attendance • Meeting guest list (inviting stakeholders) • Documentation forms • State testing • Assessment systems purchased by the district • Required district assessments • District benchmarks • District pacing guides/curricular calendars (if applicable)

Figure 2.4 Voice & Choice vs. Absence of OR Limited Voice & Choice in RtI Expanded.

There are a lot of areas where teachers have autonomy, which in turn can have a large impact on student outcomes. I believe it comes down to looking at where teachers have control — places they can make choices and use their voices — and then capitalizing on those areas. We can use these autonomy statements and turn them into high-leverage actions, creating agency. Here's what I mean:

If you can refer students to the data team, **then** there is an opportunity to create a think tank of professionals working to offer strategies and support for students.

If you can give off-cycle benchmark assessments provided by the district, **then** you can check in on students' progress and create more than one data point in which to make decisions.

If you can adjust Tier 1 instruction, daily or weekly, **then** you can respond to students' needs in real-time.

If you Increase the frequency, duration, and intensity when meeting with students, **then** you can instruct, assess, and adjust on-the-spot and in-the-moment in response to specific students.

If you create flexible, small group learning opportunities to meet students' collective and individual needs, **then** you can use proximity to lean in and listen in to students' work.

If you use students' assets to create a focus for instruction, **then** you can work off the good and capitalize on what students can do as you support students' areas needing a lift.

If you use student work products to inform instruction and guide the next steps, **then** you can add other diverse data points to the conversation versus using one data point that is typically numerical.

If you prioritize classroom set-up & design to meet students' needs, **then** you can use students' environment as an intervention in and of itself.

Using if / then statements to name intentions, followed by action-filled next steps, creates opportunities for increased autonomy and agency for both teachers and students.

WHAT CAN WE DO ABOUT IT?

If we want to honor and increase teachers' autonomy and agency, with a focus on supporting all students, we need to provide structures across the year that show our trust, admiration, and belief in teachers and the decisions they make to support students. Approaching our work with an inquiry stance — across the entire learning community — creates a culture that approaches work through a *let's figure this out* and *what can we do together* mode.

We can increase our autonomy and agency when we turn our beliefs into actions by thinking about *If...Then...* statements that have or could have a positive impact on our learning community. Take a look at these and complete the statement concerning what you know would positively benefit those you serve.

If you have a choice in how you take and record anecdotal records, **then** you
_____.

If you create ongoing, authentic formative assessments to inform instruction and guide next steps, **then** you _____
_____.

When teachers feel safe and free of judgment, they are more likely to nudge themselves and their colleagues to create new ways of looking at the day-to-day routines, creatively solve problems, and rethink original decisions when the outcomes are not what they intended. Also, teachers will ask questions and even ask others for support when figuring out different ways of meeting students' needs. In 2012, Thomas Armstrong wrote an article titled, "First, Discover Their Strengths." While the article focused on students identified with special education needs, his stance applies to all students. Armstrong (2012) urges us to think about learning through a neurodiversity lens, noting that there is no *typical* brain and because of that, we should approach our work with students "not in terms of their deficits, but primarily in terms of their strengths" (p. 10.)

This asset-based approach gives us a positive lens from which to work alongside students, making decisions to support their unique needs. While this is challenging work, it is also exciting because we open up all kinds of possibilities. We can find new ways to shore up students' misconceptions and misunderstandings and also uncover students' strengths, talents, and passions.

Questions that Inspire Inquiry Protocol

Directions: As you plan and implement instruction for students — for students who are above, at, or below grade level expectations — use these questions to guide your planning and reflection.

Questions to Ask While Planning

- What do students know (K)? What can they understand (U)? What can they do (D)? In broad strokes (generalizations) or specific to individual students, make a list and then label them with a K, U, or D.
- What do students need next? Where are they now and what is the end goal for them, whole class, small groups, or individually? What do they need to progress?
- What are students' interests? What will motivate and engage them in learning?
- As you observe and confer with students, what do you notice? How will your observations and anecdotal notes impact your instructional designs?
- What support (extensions and lifts) will you build into instructional plans based on what you know about students?
- What are you wondering about your students? How will you find the answers to your inquiries?

Questions to Ask as You Implement Plans

- How are students responding to the instructional plans you designed for them? What, if any, adjustments need to be made, in the short and long-term?
- As you observe and interact with students, what do you see and hear? Why does what you see and hear matter to student learning?

Questions to Ask After You Implement Plans

- What worked? What was clunky?
- Based on your observations and interactions with students, what are your next steps?

Taking Stock of Our Autonomy & Agency Protocol

Directions: Explain that this initial brainstorming is a safe space — all answers and thinking will be honored. The main purpose of this experience is not to build consensus, but to create an understanding and appreciation between and among stakeholders.

Step 1: Share the working definitions of autonomy and agency. Ask participants if they agree with the definitions or if they would like to tweak them.
> **AUTONOMY:** Having the capacity to act, to self-govern, to make decisions on your own. Having a feeling of empowerment and independence.
> **AGENCY:** Having the will to take action and be an agent of change.

Step 2: Create 2 separate charts and display them so that all participants can see them.

Step 3: Ask someone to be the scribe. This person will record ideas from the group.

Step 4: Ask: *Think about the time we spend at school across a day, month, and year. What do you have locus of control over? What, when, where, how, and how often do you have the autonomy (voice and choice) to make decisions about, and for your students and classroom?*

Step 5: Give participants a chance to talk about their ideas and make a list.

Step 6: Ask: *Think about the time we spend at school across a day, month, and year. What don't you have locus of control over? What, when, where, how, and how often don't you have the autonomy (voice and choice) to make decisions about, and for your students and classroom?*

Step 7: Give participants a chance to talk about their ideas and make a list.

Step 8: Once the 2 charts are co-constructed, reflect to discuss the implications for your work going forward.
- Ask: *What do you think about the 2 charts? Is there anything that makes you feel jazzed up and excited about your work? Is there anything that is worrying you? How can we use the things that we have voice and choice (autonomy) about to take action (agency) to move students forward?*

PROTOCOL

What, when, where, how, how often do you have voice and choice to make decisions about, and for your students and classroom?	What, when, where, how, how often don't you have voice and choice to make decisions about, and for your students and classroom?
• Read aloud choices • Family share nights / open houses • Instructional materials used to differentiate lessons • Field trips	• School day hours • Bell schedule • District pacing guide • State standards • Class roster
What, when, where, how, how often do you have voice and choice to make decisions about, and for your students and classroom?	**What, when, where, how, how often don't you have voice and choice to make decisions about, and for your students and classroom?**

Taking Stock of Students' Needs & Wants Protocol

PROTOCOL

Directions: One of the most important moves we can make as educators is using in-the-moment data that comes directly from students. We can gather this intel through observations, interactions, and surveys. Select and use the templates to collect data about students' assets and areas needing a lift during class. Then, after the observation, use your notes to reflect and determine the next steps.

Problem Of Practice #2

Whole Class Observation Template

Date	Student's Name	Assets	Areas Needing a Lift	What is your entry point in supporting this student? Where will you begin?

Individual Student Observation Template

Student Name _____   Date _____

When is this observation or interaction taking place? (time, class period, etc.)	Assets	Areas Needing a Lift	What is your entry point in supporting this student? Where will you begin?

PROTOCOL

Creating A Think Tank For Teachers To Study Protocol

Directions: On-going study to bolster our professional knowledge, skills, and strategies is foundational to our professional core. Use your knowledge of students, coupled with your professional knowledge and pedagogy, to complete the template. The *Recommendations* column is a place to name actions that will create movement going forward, but also a place to name things that you would like to study to create new solutions.

Think Tank Template

Questions	What do you think?	Recommendations
What assets do your students bring with them to school each day?		
Area(s) of Focus What areas are difficult for students (skills, knowledge, or understandings) and need some extra attention?		
Student Support • Who is receiving services? • How often? • Push in? • Pull out? • Some push in/pull out? • What are students missing if they are being pulled out?		
What assessments are given? • What? • When? • How often? • To whom? • By whom?		

Small-Group Work • How are groups created? • How often do they meet? • How often do they change? • Do they always meet with the teacher or are there protocols in place where they can meet sometimes without the teacher? • What work is completed during small group time?		
Paraprofessionals/ Classroom Aides • Do you have collaborative planning time together? • How are these supports utilized across the day? Week? • When, where, why, how, how often do they support students? • What do they need to support students more efficiently and effectively?		

PROTOCOL

If you would like to use this process and create your own inquiry questions, use the blank template below.

Think Tank Template (Blank)

Questions	What do you think?	Recommendations

If/Then Protocol

Directions: Create a two-column chart using the example below as a reference. You can start with the statements listed below and add ideas in the blank spaces or start with a blank template.

If/Then Template

IF...	THEN...
If you analyze how to use time that has been allocated for learning	**then** you can work to increase the amount of work time available for students to do literacy work.
If you communicate and collaborate with families	**then** together you can build an academic, social, and emotional bridge between home and school, doubling down on efforts and creating clarity of goals.
If you use technology, school library/media center resources, manipulatives, and tools	**then** you can help students go from the concrete to the abstract OR go from surface to deeper understanding.

Teacher Self-Reflection Protocol: Autonomy & Agency

Directions: The support structures we provide to students are multi-faceted. Take time to self-reflect using the questions as a guide.

Teacher Self-Reflection: Autonomy & Agency

Question	Self-Assessment					What do you need next? What are your next steps?
I/we have the autonomy, the capacity to act, to self-govern, to make decisions on my own. I/we have a feeling of empowerment and independence.	Seldom		Some of the time		Most of the time	
	1	2	3	4	5	
I/we have agency, I have the will to take action and be an agent of change.	Seldom		Some of the time		Most of the time	
	1	2	3	4	5	

What needs to happen to increase your autonomy and agency? List steps or bullet points to describe your perspective.

Autonomy	Agency

Chapter 3

PROBLEM OF PRACTICE #3:
We need child study teams focused on students' assets.

Community development officials and public health professionals are two groups of people who have been prioritizing asset-based approaches for decades. City planners take surveys asking stakeholders what types of amenities they would like to see offered as community spaces are developed. They utilize people's wants and needs, taking into account the end user's perspective as being an essential feedback loop for making plans forward. EMTs are trained to quickly respond to emergencies first by taking the patient's vitals — if there's a pulse and an unobstructed airway, they can build upon that as they triage and make a plan for restored health. While these two examples may seem simple, they are foundational because many of the practices are rooted in "working off the good" then making a plan for what should come next.

These examples focus on assets — the good that comes to the table — to build upon human, social, and cultural capital. When we focus on asset-based approaches, we spend time identifying and utilizing our individual and collective strengths, rather than focusing on deficits, or weaknesses. The big idea is to build, lead, and sustain the community by focusing on the positive contributions that already exist and then continuing to enhance, or lift, the well-being of all stakeholders.

For some communities, like a local gym, that could look like a wall of celebration focusing on milestones in goal setting, creating a congratulatory space for reflecting on an exercise journey. Or the back of the little league t-shirts sharing gratitude for the sponsorships and contributions of the program's support and development. In a school, it might be a wall of book jackets honoring the many authors and books that guide, mentor, and teach us. No matter how you slice it, all of these real-world examples focus on the good. That's because the good, even if it represents small steps, make us feel a sense of pride, accomplishment, and a path forward. No one wants to enter their local gym and see their picture next to negative statements focused on the things that went wrong during last week's workout. If that were a regular practice, people would start to talk, and eventually, that gym would have a reputation of being bucket-depleting versus bucket-filling.

Since we have a choice in which gym we belong to, if there's a deficit-approach my guess is membership would decline. In the same spirit, if t-shirts were made to highlight losing teams or if book celebration walls became places to track undesirable reading habits, engagement and commitment to the program or initiative would diminish and eventually cease. That's because people do not typically show up day-in and day-out to learn about the bad. People anchor in and show up when there is something, even the smallest thing, to hold onto that is going in a positive direction. It is human to lean into asset-based experiences and lean away from deficit-based ones.

Stakeholders in schools — students, teachers, support staff, administrators, and families are no different. They show up because schools are places that shout out, "This is a place where you can learn and get better!" Isn't that the purpose of school? To have a place — a safe, caring, supportive place — to learn and get better? I believe it is which is why I've spent the last 28 years showing up in schools because, like students, I want to learn and get better too.

How is it, then, that sometimes schools have started to lean toward a deficit-model? Some may argue that if we name what is not working or what is broken, we (teachers) can use a *fix it* approach to making things better. However, this approach is reactive instead of proactive. If schools focus on building students up, using their assets as a starting point, we create a proactive, positive stance. This "positive development emphasizes strengths over weaknesses, resilience over risk, and assets over deficits" (Rose, 2006, p. 236). Also, to prioritize equity and access for all, an asset-based approach to education is necessary. "In recent years, while equity and access efforts shined a light on marginalized and underrepresented communities, some efforts treated schools and communities like they needed to be *saved*. With an asset-based approach, every community is valuable; every community has strengths and potential" ("An Asset-Based Approach", 2018).

Schools have this kumbaya-like feeling. At least they should. While kumbaya is rooted in a religious connotation, we could change some mindsets if our day-to-day operations had a little more kumbaya in them. The word origin focuses on the idea of *come by here*. It was put into daily practice and remembered through song to convey a message of helping those in need. Schools are about helping those in need and I would argue that everyone has needs that span deep and wide because learning is never done. The more we learn, the more we know. The more we know, the more we may want or need to learn. Education is about the business of knowing more and getting better. Knowing more about our students' assets leads us to get better at leveraging their strengths in support of their overall growth and development.

NAMING THE PROBLEM

Problem Of Practice #3: We Need Child Study Teams Focused on Students' Assets.

If we are working toward knowing more and doing better, why is it, then, when we get to the data table to discuss how we will help students, the conversation turns toward the negative? Why is the majority of time spent talking about what kids cannot do versus what they can do? Why is there sometimes a pervasive culture that says if we do not shine a spotlight on students' deficits, we are not doing our job?

In this chapter, I will be referring to data team meetings as a structure for when teachers, teams, schools, and districts join together to discuss student data. As I support schools, I notice that many of these meetings have different names, but all have similar characteristics. Here's a quick look at what I mean.

Other Names for Data Team Meetings	Common Characteristics
• Child Study Teams • Team Data Meetings • Literacy Team • Numeracy Team • RtI Data Meetings • AIS Data Meetings	• Meet regularly to discuss student data • Data is a major component of the meeting • Someone is in charge of leading the meeting • Majority of meeting time discusses what has been done in the past for "low" students

Figure 3.1 Other Names for Data Team Meetings / Common Characteristics.

HAVE WE CREATED A DEFICIT-FOCUSED DATA CULTURE?

I have two important things to mention here. First, I am not into scapegoating. I am especially not into scapegoating when kids, and their growth and development, are at stake. Second, I am teachers' number one fan! I was a classroom teacher for fifteen years, and for the past thirteen years, I have served as an instructional coach and educational consultant supporting teachers' work each day. Teachers want the best for their students. The more you know and work with teachers, the more that becomes a universal truth. I say all of this to explain that even though I get teachers and I get schools, something doesn't feel quite right. Somehow, in some way, I believe a deficit-seeking data culture has been created. It's not any one person or organization or local, state, or federal mandate's fault. It's a combination of factors. It's in our collective best interest to name it as an issue, then create new or revised practices to move toward a more asset-based stance. In simple terms: It is time for us to knock it off — replacing our deficit stance to an asset-based stance and do better.

If you are not sure what I mean, here are some examples of the language and actions that show up when we operate from a deficit-seeking culture. You might hear:

- "He's sooooooo looooow. I have done everything I know to do, and nothing is working."
- "I called the mom. She said she doesn't know what to do either. If the mom cannot deal with it, how can we?"
- "If you can just take her out of the classroom during reading, that would be great. She cannot do any of the work anyways and needs something different."
- "I am not really a reading teacher. Kids used to come to me already knowing how to read. I just do not know what has happened to these kids. Maybe video games or lack of parent involvement is the root cause of the issues."
- "I cannot manage small group work because the kids just are not ready for it. They cannot really handle it; they just are not independent enough."
- "I had her brother in my class a few years ago. It is no surprise that she is struggling. She is behind in almost everything and is doing the best she can do. Maybe we should adjust our expectations for her?"
- "He says he's just bored. I told him he could take the advanced English

class if he wanted to take the placement test, but he just shrugged his shoulders. I feel like he's just lazy."
- "Look at all of the data on the spreadsheet that is red (not meeting expectations). I have done everything the same as in years past, and those kids did not struggle. This class is just lower."

There may be some statements you can relate to, for one reason or another. If you are like me, at some point in your teaching career you may have thought or said something similar. Your intentions were good — maybe you were worn out or worn down — and releasing some emotion and stress related to your worry list was needed. Maybe colleagues around you speak that way regularly and that mindset is part of your school culture. It happens even to the best of people and schools, with the best intentions. Regardless, what's important is recognizing it and working to find more positive solutions. One way to maintain an asset-based stance is to name our beliefs and then work to put those beliefs into asset-based actions.

THIS I BELIEVE

This I Believe (What do you believe?)	**I Will** (How does this show up in your work?)
Data team meetings should be used as a child study process where multiple data points are included, especially data that focuses on students' assets.	Do not rely solely on numerical data, collect multi-faceted data focused on students' interests, passions, wants, strengths, and needs.
Studying students, and taking an inquiry approach to knowing them well, across settings and days gives us up-to-date data at our fingertips.	Use kidwatching strategies to take note of students' work products, actions, inactions, and interactions and making sure that asking questions that lead to further study and kidwatching is included (Wright & Hoonan, 2019).
Asking students what they need, as part of the data gathering process, is essential.	Create systems and structures for getting students' input on their interests, passions, wants, strengths, and needs and use that data in our responses.
Less time sitting in data meetings talking about the past, potentially running out of time, more time talking about actions forward.	Create a protocol or develop an agenda that gives the bulk of the meeting time to creating a plan of action.

Figure 3.2 This I Believe / I Will.

GOING FROM DEFICIT-BASED TO ASSET-BASED

Think about this quote, which was adapted from a Sweedish Proverb that says, "In any piece of text, the best is between the lines." (www.goodreads.com) I love this quote and the meaning it brings forth. While it speaks to written text, I believe it can be applied to the *text* that lies around our students. Barry Hoonan and I write about *Kidwatching 2.0* (Wright & Hoonan, 2019). We urge teachers to lean on the early literacy practice and term coined by Owocki and Goodman (2002) called *kidwatching*. The big ideas behind Kidwatching 2.0 focus on studying students across classes/subjects, through different lenses, and from multiple perspectives. In the classroom, we gather kidwatching intel, or data, that we can use to inform our next moves. It can be as simple as creating a two-column chart where we can capture what students know, understand, and can do and then noting any wonderings we have based on our observations. I call this, *Roaming in the Known* and *Roaming in the Wonderings*. It means that we are up on our feet, circulating around the classroom or learning environment, and catching all of the things students are up to. Whether we are focusing on one student or studying a small group, this process leads to an inquiry stance from the get-go. Here's a template that you can use to collect observations and wonderings.

Student	Roaming in the Known (What do students know, understand, and can do?)	Roaming in the Wonderings (As I study and observe, what do I wonder?)

Figure 3.3 Roaming in the Known / Roaming in the Wonderings.

If we study students — social-emotionally, academically, and physically — and use that intel to guide our next steps, then we must read between the lines or we will miss some of the most important information. There is no one right way to study students, and there are lots of ways you can use the tools at your fingertips to collect data in organized ways. One simple way is to jot observational notes about:
- What is the student up to?
- What did we learn?

As you read these scenarios, imagine putting yourself in the teachers' or teams' shoes. You might even consider putting yourself in the student's or family's shoes.

As you read the first scenario, ask yourself:
- Do you know a student who shares some similar strengths or areas of need as the student being described?
  If so,
    - How did you approach the work?
    - What data did you collect?
  If not,
    - How would you approach the work?

○ What data do you think would be beneficial to collect?

Scenario 1

We have concerns about a student's reading progress. We study him across several reading workshops, and we have not learned what we need to create our next steps. So, we decided to study this student's reading across other content areas. We study:

What is the student up to?	What did we learn?
Reading a piece of sheet music during choir	• Student uses his finger to follow along • Student asks peer for help when he gets lost in the pace of the piece
Reading (viewing) a demonstration of how to serve a volleyball during P.E. class	• Student watches demonstration, tried it out himself and finds success
Reading the lunch line "Specials of the Day" board and listening in as the student interacts with the lunchroom staff	• Student talks to a friend about lunch choices • Student asks lunchroom staff if certain items can be substituted so that he can get a double helping of crispy fries

Figure 3.4 What Are Students Up To?

Given what you now know about this student, what do you think?
- What inferences can you make about the students' strengths based on this information?
- What other data would you want to collect to get a fuller picture of the students' strengths and areas of need?
- Where and when would you work to collect the data?

Our team was able to study this student across multiple settings and it gave us a fuller view of this student's reading strengths and areas where he may need a lift. From this, we concluded that this student:
- Uses strategies for seeking help when he is confused by collaborating with a peer
- Finds success by watching a demonstration and then having time to practice what he just saw

- Enjoys interaction with others, especially talking out needs and wants

This data was helpful during future reading instruction. It led to supporting this student by:
- Creating a thinking partnership with another student — someone to check in with when confused
- Inviting him to watch a quick, strategic minilesson and then a short practice session
- Scheduling or encouraging talk time with others to name and solidify things he is thinking about

As you read the second scenario, ask yourself:
- How much time across a week should students write? What feels like the "right" amount?
- What does it look, sound and feel like when students write with independence? Does that change based on the grade, age, or development of the student? If so, how and why?

Scenario 2

We have concerns about a 6th grade student's writing progress. When given time to write, she finishes quickly. Writing volume is lacking. We study this student across several days of writing workshops and have a hunch that the systems and structures we currently have in place are not what the student needs.

Given what you now know about this student, what are you wondering? Consider using an asset-based stance and/or choose asset-based language to name your wonderings when answering:
- What questions do you have?
- If you were part of this team, what might you offer or suggest concerning:
  - Classroom design?
  - Curriculum, instruction, and/or assessment design?
  - Peer interactions / social engagement opportunities?
- What inquiries does this create for a professional study?

Our team gathered and posed some questions. We wondered:
- Is the notebook, paper size, or orientation the right fit for this student?
- Would other writing tools make a difference?
- Would utilizing the voice function on the computer create different re-

sults?
- Is this struggle rooted in forming ideas or getting ideas from brain to paper?

Sometimes our wonderings and inquiries can lead to theories. If, for example, we believe the paper size might be the wrong match for the student, we can create an action step that includes making a change, and ultimately testing our theory. In our meeting, it might sound like this:

"I wonder if the notebook or paper size is wrong for this student? If we offer up a variety of notebook types and paper choices, would that make a difference in how much she writes?" If we think that is a viable action step to test out our theory, we can make a quick plan to give it a go.

Here's what our action plan looked like:

What theories do we have about this student based on recent instruction?		
I wonder if the notebook or paper size is wrong for this student? If we offer up a variety of notebook types and paper choices, would that make a difference in how much she writes?		
Reflecting (What will we do differently?)	**Naming** (What is the student up to?)	**Reflecting** (What did we learn?)
Share with all students that we have put out some new notebook types and paper sizes with different orientations that can be used during the writing workshop.	The student went from using a 3 subject composition notebook to choosing loose-leaf paper with bigger lines and a space that invites a graphic or illustration.	The student started to draw a small image before writing and then went back and added details to the drawing after drafting.

Offer different size pencil lead and erasable pens for students to use when drafting.	The student went back and forth between her typical pencil and an erasable pen. She did color the image she drew with colored pencils and outlined it with a thin black sharpie.	The student was intentional about the tool she used. While this was a drafting process, her picture took the shape of a final draft. She was invested in this work and wrote more for this writing project than she has written in weeks.
Give students 5 writing topic options instead of 2 so that we can study whether writing volume for this student is tied to choice in the topic more than issues rooted in forming ideas and getting them from the brain to paper.	The student jumped right into the writing process, using one of the 5 choices given.	The student likes choice — choice in paper, choice in tools, choice in topic. The student most likely does not have struggles with writing. We need to keep an eye on her, but mostly we need to adjust what we are doing and the choices we are offering.

Figure 3.5 Action Plan.

If we isolate our observations and only use the data we find during a specific time, our solutions may be short-sighted. That is why looking beyond what is right in front of us, by "looking between the lines", gives us a chance to see a fuller data picture from which to base theories and create solutions to the problems of practice we face when supporting students.

WHAT CAN WE DO ABOUT IT?

I'm not here to tell you whether you or your organization needs a total reboot or a slight adjustment. I believe that work has to start at the individual level and works its way through the system. What I do know is that it's time for a change. We can no longer look at, talk about, or interact with students using deficit thinking. To do so creates inequities and puts students at risk. According to the National Equity Project, educational equity means: Each

child receives what they need to develop to their full academic and social potential. Working toward equity in schools involves:
- Ensuring equally high outcomes for all participants in our educational system; removing the predictability of success or failures that currently correlates with any social or cultural factor;
- Interrupting inequitable practices, examining biases, and creating inclusive multicultural school environments for adults and children; and
- Discovering and cultivating the unique gifts, talents, and interests that every human possesses. (National Equity Project, n.d.)

To create change in our schools, I suggest asking:

- When speaking about students and their work, what language is used? What types of words are used to describe what we see and hear?
- What policies, procedures, and rules are currently in play? Are they inclusive or exclusive? Do they create equitable opportunities for students or roadblocks?
- Have we ensured that the neediest and those at risk are placed in classrooms with the most highly qualified teachers?
- When we make decisions with and for students, do our plans take into account their identities, talents, interests, wants, and needs?

Shifting a culture from deficit-based to asset-based can happen if we focus:
1. Individually — looking within to take stock of our language, actions, and biases
2. Collectively — looking within our school, district or organization to take stock of our language, actions, biases, and policies
3. Collaboratively — looking outside of our school, district, or organization for guidance when needed

When we take stock, it nudges us to read, watch, listen to, and interact with others who might be able to guide us to do better or do more or make necessary changes. The ultimate goal is to change our mindset and change our policies so that they afford ALL children with equitable, educational opportunities that are culturally responsive to students' unique wants and needs. When we make commitments to increase actions that focus on students' assets, we have a greater chance to influence the whole learning community's culture for the better. At the onset, we have to think about the type of data we are bringing to the table. Bringing data that can be used to take action — not just about students, but also information about families, teachers, and teaching practices helps inform our moves forward. To create data meetings/child study teams focused on students' assets which includes multidimensional data, let's consider actions we can increase (do more of) and actions we can decrease (do less of). Here's an example:

Increase / Do More	Decrease / Do Less
Creating child study teams with multiple data points, using both qualitative and quantitative data, and with a focus on students' assets.	Talking about students, with a major focus on quantitative data, while focusing on deficits.
Using an inquiry approach and being curious about what students know and can do.	Labeling students using language that creates a fixed mindset (i.e. so low, SPED kid, high flyer).
Using conversations with students and students' self-reflection as a primary source of data to help guide decisions and action steps forward.	Using single data points to make decisions and actions to step forward.
Creating data team meeting structures focusing on actions forward versus reliving the past.	One and done data team meetings.
Working with families as partners in students' learning journey.	Blaming families for students' struggles and allowing that stance to stand in the way of working together in the service of students.

Figure 3.6 Increase / Do More vs. Decrease / Do Less.

When we focus on assets, we give ourselves and our students a chance to live in the good. By focusing on the good, we often bring out the best in ourselves and others because we bring together our individual and collective strengths. Doing so is not to neglect the areas where we need a lift or support, it just gives us a head start because we launch into the work with a positive, bucket-filling, *I can* stance. Students and adults alike show up for that kind of work because they are part of the process and can feel the growth as it happens.

Data Meetings Focused on Action Steps Forward Protocol

Directions: Too often data team meetings are filled with more time sharing about the issues and less time spent on action-oriented solutions. To help shift meeting time to focus on action steps forward, try using this time allotment for data team meetings and child study teams.

Say: The goal of this meeting structure is to meet more regularly to share updates and action steps, and to be more efficient and effective in our collective efforts.

- → 1st Meeting (30 minutes)
    - ◆ Share (10 minutes)
    - ◆ Create a plan of action (15 minutes)
    - ◆ Wrap up/next steps (5 minutes)
- → 2nd Meeting (20 minutes)
    - ◆ Share (10 minutes)
    - ◆ Create revisions to the plan of action (15 minutes)
    - ◆ Wrap up/next steps (5 minutes)
- → 3rd Meeting (20 minutes)
    - ◆ Share (10 minutes)
    - ◆ Create revisions to the plan of action (15 minutes)
    - ◆ Wrap up/next steps (5 minutes)

Meetings Focused on an Inquiry Versus Deficit Stance Protocol

Directions: To shift a meeting from a deficit stance to an inquiry stance, use this process to help shape or reshape the meeting culture by asking questions that bring out the best in everyone — students and adults alike.

Step 1: Schedule a meeting. As part of the invitation, ask participants to be ready to share 2-3 assets about each student they would like to discuss at the upcoming meeting.

Step 2: Gather participants. Pose some of these sentences as a way to begin talking about students using an inquiry stance while also focused on students' assets:

- → 2-3 assets I know about _____ are...
- → 2-3 actions I have taken to bolster _____'s assets are...
- → I wonder if _____ needs _____?
- → I wonder if we did more of _____ and less of _____, what kind of results we might find?
- → 2-3 things I think we could do to lift _____ are...
- → Some numerical data that shows _____'s strengths are...
- → Some anecdotal data that shows _____'s strengths are...
- → Some numerical data shows _____'s areas needing a lift are...
- → Some anecdotal data shows _____'s areas needing a lift are...

Step 3: Based on the data shared, make a list of the action steps going forward.

What actions will we take to bolster _____'s assets and help support areas needing a lift?

Step 4: Before the close of this meeting, schedule the next meeting (2-3 weeks) where reflections from these actions will be shared.

Ask: How long should we put our action steps into play before we meet again?
- 1 week?
- 2 weeks?
- 3 weeks?

Meetings Focused on an Inquiry Versus Deficit Stance Template

Who (Who will take action?)	**Actions** (What will we do?)	**Intended Consequences or Outcomes** (What do we anticipate will happen?)	**Future Data Collection** (What data will we collect to know if our actions proved beneficial?)

Roaming in the Known & the Wonderings Protocol

Directions: Create a two-column chart (either in your notebook or digitally) using the example below as a reference. Determine how many students you will study and decide when and where you will be kidwatching.

Time: 30 minutes total (5 minutes to get organized, 15 minutes to kidwatch, 10 minutes to talk to colleagues about findings and create next steps).

Audience: Teachers, support staff, administrators, and others serving on the student's team.

Step 1: Share this template with participants.

Step 2: During the initial data team meeting, work through the template using one student as an example. This will allow data team participants to practice using the template.

Step 3: Determine who you will kidwatch, when, and where you will collect your data.

Step 4: Meet to share findings and create the next steps.

Roaming in the Known & the Wonderings Template

Student	Roaming in the Known What do students know, understand, and can do?	Roaming in the Wonderings As I study and observe, what do I wonder?

What Are Students Up To? Protocol

Directions: Create a two-column chart using the example below as a reference. Determine how many students you will study and decide when and where you will be kidwatching.

Time: 30 minutes total (5 minutes to get organized, 15 minutes to kidwatch, 10 minutes to talk to colleagues about findings and create next steps).

Audience: Teachers, support staff, administrators, and others serving on the student's team.

Step 1: Share this template with participants.

Step 2: During the initial data team meeting, work through the template using one student as an example. This will allow data team participants to practice using the template.

Step 3: Determine who you will kidwatch, when, and where you will collect your data.

Step 4: Meet to share findings and create the next steps.

What Are Students Up To?

What are students up to?	What did we learn?

Reflecting—Naming—Reflecting Protocol

Directions: Gather the data team and create a three-column chart. Note: I suggest providing 2 versions of the chart for documenting reflections, decisions, and actions.

Materials: Chart paper and sticky notes

Round 1: Name or explain a status update at the top of the chart. What theories do we have about this student based on recent instruction?

Round 2: Participants write ideas in the left-hand column, naming actions that will be done differently and in response to the theories we just named.

Round 3: Study, or kidwatch, in the classroom to collect more data. Write these ideas in the middle column.

Round 4: Meet to share findings. Explain what we learned based on our reflections and observations. Write ideas in the right-hand column.

Note: Repeat this process multiple times for a deeper and multi-faceted conversation.

Reflecting—Naming—Reflecting Template

Status Update: What theories do we have about this student based on recent instruction?		
Reflecting (What will we do differently?)	**Naming** (What is the student up to?)	**Reflecting** (What did we learn?)

Do More / Do Less Protocol

Directions: Create a two-column chart (either with chart paper or digitally) using the example below as a reference. You can start with the ideas listed below and add on in the blank spaces or start with a blank template.

Do More / Do Less

Question: To create data meetings/child study teams focused on students' assets, what do we need to increase (do more of) and decrease (do less of)?

Increase / Do More	Decrease / Do Less
Creating child study teams with multiple data points and with a focus on students' assets.	Talking about students while focusing on deficits.
Using an inquiry approach and being curious about what students know and can do.	Labeling students using language that creates a fixed mindset [i.e. so low, SPED kid, high flyer]
Using conversations with students and students' self-reflection as a primary source of data to help guide decisions and action steps forward.	Using single data points to make decisions and action steps to move forward.
Creating data team meeting structures focusing on actions forward versus reliving the past.	One and done data team meetings.
Working with families as partners in students' learning journey.	Blaming families for students' struggles and allowing that stance to stand in the way of working together in the service of students.

What's Our Response?

Assessing & Responding to Student Numeracy Data Protocol

Directions: Project an electronic version of the template for all members of the team to view. Provide a hard or soft blank copy of the template if needed. Use the template to answer these guiding questions:
- What does the student's numeracy profile tell us?
- To date, what is the student's numeracy narrative?
- What are the student's assets?
- Where does the student need a lift?

Time: 20-25 minutes

Audience: Teachers and support staff (and anyone participating in a data team meeting)

Step 1: During the data team meeting, work through the template using one student as an example. This will allow data team participants to practice using the template.

Step 2: Ask participants if they have any other data they believe should be included in the template. Make revisions as needed.

Step 3: Create shared agreements with participants about focusing on student assets first, before discussing areas needing a lift.

Step 4: If applicable, pose the following questions to deepen thinking and planning to support students.
- What instruction is needed?
- What resource(s) will be used?
- Who will provide the instruction?
- When will the instruction be provided?
- Where will the instruction take place?
- How often will the instruction take place?

Assessing & Responding to Student Numeracy Data Template

Student Information

Name:

Current Grade:

Birthday:

Background (family/home, educational history)	**Social/Emotional**

Tier 1 Instructional Focus	Assessment Data
	Describe the student's numeracy journey and assets. What are his/her likes? Dislikes? Interests? When, where, and how does the student's numeracy excitement & joy show up?

Developmental Math Assessment

Grade Level	Number Concepts	Operations	Geometry	Measurement	Data

Standards for Mathematical Practice

Make sense of problems and persevere in solving them	
Reason abstractly and quantitatively	
Construct viable arguments and critique the reasoning of others	
Model with mathematics	
Use appropriate tools strategically	
Attend to precision	
Look for and make use of structure	
Look for and express regularity in repeated reasoning	

Other

Teacher Observations:

Other Assessments:

Student Work Samples: See attached

PROTOCOL

Problem of Practice #3

Tier 2 Instructional Focus	Related Services

Assessing & Responding to Student Literacy Data Protocol

Directions: Project an electronic version of the template for all members of the team to view. Provide a hard or soft blank copy of the template if needed. Use the template to answer these guiding questions:
- What does the student's literacy profile tell us?
- To date, what is the student's literacy narrative?
- What are the student's assets?
- Where does the student need a lift?

Time: 20-25 minutes

Audience: Teachers and support staff (and anyone participating in a data team meeting)

Step 1: During the data team meeting, work through the template using one student as an example. This will allow data team participants to practice using the template.

Step 2: Ask participants if they have any other data they believe should be included in the template. Make revisions as needed.

Step 3: Create shared agreements with participants about focusing on student assets first, before discussing areas needing a lift.

Step 4: If applicable, pose the following questions to deepen thinking and planning to support students.
- What instruction is needed?
- What resource(s) will be used?
- Who will provide the instruction?
- When will the instruction be provided?
- Where will the instruction take place?
- How often will the instruction take place?

Assessing and Responding to Student Literacy Data Template

Student Background	
Student's Name:	Preferred Pronoun:
Teacher(s):	Grade Level:
Support Teacher(s):	Language(s): Encoding/Decoding
Handedness:	Birthday:
Glasses/Corrective Lenses:	Today's Date:

Developmental Reading, Writing, and Word Study Data	State Testing Data	Other Numerical Data

Asset-Based Observations			
(observe the student at different times of day, across different settings and collect asset-based observational evidence)			
Observation #1 When: Where:	**Observation #2** When: Where:	**Observation #3** When: Where:

Other Data
(observe what you see/hear OR take note after conferring with student)

Texts in "Up Next to Read" Pile	Favorite Color	Slow Starter or Quick on Feet	On the Talkative or Quiet Side
Biggest Fear/Worry	**Good Friend(s)**	**Favorite Thing to Do in Free Time**	**Stay Up Late or Go to Bed Early**
Homework Lover or Hater	**Favorite Fruit or Vegetable**	**Favorite Place to be Calm**	**Favorite Place to be Rowdy**
Beach or Snow	**Test Anxiety**	**What Does a Teacher Need to Know About You to Support You**	**One Word to Describe Yourself**

PROTOCOL

PROTOCOL

Patterns/Generalization (based on what you observed, fill in the 2-column chart below)	
Student Assets	**Areas Needing a *Lift***

Plan Of Action (make a plan to support the student)		
Who	**What Is The Plan?**	**Frequency, Duration, Intensity**
Teacher		
Support Staff		
Grade Level Team		
Administrator(s)		
Other		

What's Our Response?

Teacher Self-Reflection Protocol: Asset-Based Child Study Teams

Directions: The support structures we provide to students are multi-faceted. Take time to self-reflect using the question as a guide.

Teacher Self-Reflection: Asset-Based Child Study Teams

Question	Self-Assessment					What do you need next? What are your next steps?
I/we have created child study teams focused on students' assets.	Seldom		Some of the time		Most of the time	
	1	2	3	4	5	

What needs to happen to ensure asset-based child study teams? List steps or bullet points to describe your perspective.

Asset-Based Child Study Teams

Problem of Practice #3

Chapter 4

PROBLEM OF PRACTICE #4:
We need to increase students' thinking and doing time.

Teachers show up each day to do good by kids. After working in schools for many years, I'm certain of that. Teachers are well-intentioned, service-oriented people who want to impact the lives of their students. When best, enduring practices or timely strategies are not being implemented, it is usually not a lack of desire, but rather a lack of know-how.

During coaching sessions, I often ask teachers to name their beliefs. The focus area is dependent on the goals of our work together, but often beliefs about education or learning, student engagement, and motivation, formative and summative assessment, or data becomes a focal point. When teachers share their beliefs with me, I ask them to also share how their beliefs show up in their work. Heidi Mills and Tim O'Keefe (2015) wrote an essay where they assert, "The beliefs we hold as teachers matter. They always have and they always will. Whether we realize it or not, our beliefs underpin the moves we make as teachers, regardless of where or whom we teach. Beliefs also serve as the catalyst for, or limitations of, professional growth and change" (p. 31). In practice, there is often a distance between what we say we believe and our know-how in putting those beliefs into action. That is a natural part of growth.

Let's think about a different example. I like yoga. I think I could be a yoga instructor someday. However, I currently take a yoga class where the participants are over the age of 70, and they are more skilled than I am. I love the class because it invigorates me. I tell myself, *if they can do it, then I can too*! I believe I can be a yoga instructor, but there is a distance between what I believe and my being able to take action on those beliefs. I cannot instruct a yoga class, yet. But, I can work to put my beliefs into action and close the distance between what I know and what I can do.

Often, there are commonalities among teachers' beliefs. For example, when teachers name their beliefs about education or learning, they often write about:
- Classroom community
- Rigorous student work
- Student motivation and engagement
- Student-centered pedagogy
- Assessment
- Equal access to resources
- Diversity
- Inclusivity

MEET MADISON

Madison is a seventh grade ELA and Social Studies teacher and has taught for ten years. She loves middle schoolers, is a co-advisor of the schools' student council and coaches the girls' basketball team. Here are Madison's beliefs:
- Students need to be heard. They need opportunities to share their thoughts and learn from one another because they have important things to contribute.
- Everyone in our learning community matters.
- Classrooms need to be a safe space for students to learn and share.
- Formative assessments guide our steps forward.
- Students need to read and write a lot in all classes to grow as readers, writers, and thinkers.

To visualize Madison's classroom, you have to imagine a medium-sized, rectangular classroom with desks in rows facing a wall-length whiteboard. In the back corner, there is a teacher's desk and chair, and in the other corner, there is a circular table that seats four. Along one wall there are two bookshelves filled with novels. Madison's forty-eight minute class period starts with a bell ringer, followed by a mostly lecture-based experience, and typically ends with an exit ticket or homework reminders. Sometimes, toward the middle of the class period, Madison's students turn and talk or share ideas. This is the typical structure from day-to-day, except Thursday or Friday when students take some type of assessment.

As Madison's instructional coach, it is not my job to try and change her. It is my job to support her reach her goals and help her put her beliefs into action in the service of student growth. In that spirit, I suggested to Madison that we study how we are using the instructional time allotted for her classes across the week and look at how we can use that time to boost her beliefs into overdrive. At the time, I am not sure Madison completely understood this suggested plan, but since we have a trusting, collegial relationship, she was agreeable. I also knew that we would be studying together and that Madison would be in the driver's seat so this was a safe space for us to use an inquiry stance to move forward.

To get started, I made this chart in my notebook focused on Madison's beliefs:

This I Believe (What do you believe?)	I Will (How does this show up in your work?)
Students need to be heard. They need opportunities to share their thoughts and learn from one another because they have important things to contribute.	
Everyone in our learning community matters.	
Classrooms need to be a safe space for students to learn and share.	
Formative assessments guide our steps forward.	
Students need to read and write a lot in all classes to grow as readers, writers, and thinkers.	

Figure 4.1 Madison's This I Believe.

I have supported a lot of amazing teachers over the years. In that time, I have learned that taking stock of how time is being used is important because time is a hot commodity and often directly related to supporting teachers' goals, whether formally or informally. For example, if Madison believes, "Students need to read and write a lot in all classes to grow as readers, writers, and thinkers," then students need a lot of time to read and write. Because Madison believes that, "Students need to be heard. They need opportunities to share their thoughts and learn from one another...," students will need time during the class period to share often. From experience, I know that if we use a lecture-based structure less, we can increase students' thinking and doing time. When we hand more learning time over to students, there are many benefits which include increased time to:

- Read
- Write
- Work in small groups (with or without the teacher)
- Work 1:1 (teacher to student)
- Differentiate
- Collaborate
- Work at own pace
- Students being in charge of learning instead of waiting for learning to happen

NAMING THE PROBLEM

Problem Of Practice #4: We Need to Increase Students' Thinking and Doing Time.

Samantha Bennett, friend and author of *That Workshop Book,* talks about the ways people of all ages learn. She always says, "the person who is doing the reading, writing, and thinking is the one who is doing the learning" (Bennett, 2007). I also believe that to be true. When we take stock of how instructional time is being used across the class period and school day, week, and year, we can address this challenge by comparing the amount of teacher talk time with the amount of student thinking and doing time. Learners must be doers, taking an active stance in the learning so that they get the full value out of the experience. Therefore, about how instructional time is being allocated and used, there should be an imbalance, handing more of the time over to students. In other words, by decreasing teacher talk time, we increase students' think-time, talk-time, and work-time.

Here are my beliefs that relate to honor students' thinking and doing time.

THIS I BELIEVE

This I Believe (What do you believe?)	**I Will** (How does this show up in your work?)
Taking stock of the allotted instructional time gives us insights into how time is currently being used so that we can make desired adjustments.	With a shared agreement among teachers, study how time is being used across instructional periods. Then, use that data to help guide collaborative decision-making and the next steps.
Keeping minilessons (or direct instruction time) short gives more time for students to work independently, in small groups, or one-on-one with the teacher.	Use collaborative, co-planning templates and routines to plan instruction that gives students 2/3 of the instructional time to do the work.
When we hand over more of the learning time to students, we have to "size up" the types of work they will be engaging in so that we ensure rigorous, meaningful work.	Use protocols for studying student work.
When students have opportunities to think, talk, and work about real-world products for authentic audiences, students' motivation, engagement, and buy-in increases.	Use mentor texts as real-world models and create opportunities for students to share work products with authentic audiences when co-planning.

Figure 4.2 This I Believe / I Will.

CLOSING THE GAP BETWEEN BELIEFS AND PRACTICES

When working with teachers, I often say, "We have to name it to change it." We cannot change something unless we begin by naming it. Before I elaborate, it is important to note that "change" does not imply that something is wrong. A change could be doing what is already good, and changing it by doing it more often. As a result, we can make a change by:
- Adding something new to our routines and practices
- Doing something more often
- Doing something differently
- Doing something less often
- Eliminating something from our routines and practices

I asked Madison to think about the beliefs she named and explain how they show up or could show up in her practice. Here's what she shared:

This I Believe (What do you believe?)	I Will (How does this show up in your work?)
Students need to be heard. They need opportunities to share their thoughts and learn from one another because they have important things to contribute.	• Turn & Talk • Talk time at the beginning & end of class • Collaborative projects
Everyone in our learning community matters.	• Positive classroom behavior • Mutual respect
Classrooms need to be a safe space for students to learn and share.	• Positive classroom behavior • Norms for sharing (in-person & digital)
Formative assessments guide our steps forward.	• Assessments at least one time per week (usually Thursday or Friday) • Use the data for grades and intervention/extra help during study hall
Students need to read and write a lot to grow as readers and writers.	• Silent reading on Mondays • Silent reading when students finish work early • Free Write Fridays

Figure 4.3 Madison's This I Believe and I Will.

After she shared her ideas, I asked Madison if she had one or two that she wanted to focus on. We talked about possibilities — what we could add, do more of, do differently, do less of, and/or eliminate.

As Madison shared, I jotted some notes. Here is what I learned:

This I Believe (What do you believe?)	I Will (How does this show up in your work?)	Making Changes How would you like to make a change? (select one or two)
Students need to be heard. They need opportunities to share their thoughts and learn from one another because they have important things to contribute.	• Turn & Talk • Talk time at the beginning & end of class • Collaborative projects	• Adding something new to our routines and practices • Doing something more often
Students need to read and write a lot to grow as readers and writers.	• Silent reading on Mondays • Silent reading when students finish work early • Free Write Fridays	• Doing something differently

Figure 4.4 Madison's This I Believe, I Will and Making Changes.

Madison explained that she likes students to *Turn & Talk*, but that she thinks they should do that more often. She explained that if students do that more often, they might get tired of it. We discussed that adding something new to the sharing routine could be something that we work on together. Through conversation, I learned that Madison was agreeable to students trying out some new sharing protocols as long as she and I could try them out together.

Additionally, Madison shared that she has students read silently on Monday in hopes that they will get into the book they are reading and continue reading more across the week at home. Admittedly, she explained that reading only on Mondays is probably not enough. She said she would like to do something different that would give students opportunities to read more in school.

Working with Madison is a great example of how important it is for teachers to have a thinking partner. Thinking Partnerships create many big takeaways, including:
- Promoting risk-taking and trust
- Igniting thinking to get ideas on the table before, during and after a learning experience

- Provoking divergent thinking by pairing learners who may bring out new ideas by working together
- Building new relationships OR building up existing relationships
- Creating a culture of continued learning and revision (Wright, 2019)

Together, Madison and I were able to use her beliefs and her current practices as a starting point for making change. And, even though it was not named directly, some of the changes she made had a direct impact on increasing students' thinking and doing time. Read on to see how.

WHAT CAN WE DO ABOUT IT?

If the goal is to increase students' thinking and doing time, we have to study and take stock of the ways we are using the time we have. Then, we can find ways to bolster what is working and replace practices that are not yielding the desired results. Here is a 4-step process, using my beliefs, as a backdrop for increasing students' thinking and doing time.

1. Take stock of the allotted instructional time.
2. Keep minilessons (or direct instruction time) to a minimum, approximately 9-11 minutes, giving students the majority of the instructional time to work.
3. Stand back, reflect, and "size up" the types of work students will be engaging in so that we ensure rigorous, meaningful work.
4. Share real-world products with students to use as mentor texts and co-create authentic audience opportunities with whom students can share.

When we **take stock of allotted instructional time**, we are committing to studying how we use the time we have across several days. Teachers can study their own time or they can work collaboratively to study across their classrooms. At the start of the class period, note the time and take stock of what the teacher and the students are up to. Across the class period, continue to note the time and observations. When making observations, remember this is an asset-based protocol meaning that observations should assume best intentions and capture the good that is occurring across the classroom. Then, analyze how time was used by asking:

- Who did the majority of talking and doing? Teachers? Students?
- What was the teacher's role across the class period?
- What were the students' roles across the class period?
- If we want or need to shift more time to students, when, where, and how

can we accomplish that goal?

Have you ever wondered why the typical TedTalk is approximately 18 minutes long? That is because the TED curator, Chris Anderson, explains it is "long enough to be serious and short enough to hold people's attention and say something that matters" (Gallo, 2015). Ask teachers across the globe how long students' attention spans are and you will hear a common response: Not long. Educational action-research, through observations and experiences, has taught us that we have approximately 9-20 minutes to access students' optimal attention span. Put another way, kids cannot sit and listen to a teacher, and remain focused, for more than 20 minutes at a given time. To do this, make a plan for **keeping minilessons (or direct instruction) short so that students have more time to work independently, in small groups or one-on-one with the teacher.** An easy, at-your-fingertips strategy is to set a timer and keep instruction within the allotted time.

If you take stock of the allotted instructional time and set a timer so that you keep minilessons short, strategic, and succinct, students will have more work time. It is important to make sure that we maximize their learning time by **ensuring that students are engaging in rigorous, meaningful work.** You can "size up" student work by asking:
- Is student work connected to the big picture / guiding questions?
- Does the student work represent the "sweet spot" for students — challenging without creating frustration?
- Do students know the why behind what they are learning and how their work products represent their evolving knowledge, skills, and understandings?
- Does the student work resemble work products that could be found in the real-world?
- Can students reflect on their work products and explain how they can transfer the learning from one experience to another?

BUILDING ON SUCCESSES

Remember how Madison said, "Students need to be heard...because they have important things to contribute?" You may recall that her students were already using Turn & Talk to share ideas. We made an effort to do more of that, across the instructional periods and weeks. Madison also wanted to add something new to her sharing routine. Together we worked to create small, flexible sharing groups two times per week. This time gave students opportunities to share drafts of work products, reflections, connections, aha moments, and give one another asset-based feedback.

Madison also wanted students to read and write a lot, and she explained that she wanted to do something differently. Madison decided to rename *Silent Reading* on Mondays to *Choice Reading & Writing* on Monday, Wednesday and Friday. With the addition of this structure, Madison's students had 15 minutes, three times per week, to read or write whatever they wanted. Since Madison also teaches Social Studies, we created a new structure during that instructional period called, *Teach Me Tuesdays*. Each Tuesday students would choose from a few short text types (newspaper articles, short video clips, infographics) related to a historical topic. Students would:
- Select 1-2 short texts to read
- Read for 15 minutes
- Share new ideas or interesting points with a small group

This structure gave students an opportunity to increase reading and talking volume. Often, because the short text topics were interesting, it also piqued students' interests which led to more reading outside of the class. I would be remiss to mention that in addition to these changes, Madison also gave students a choice in whom they would read, write, and share with across her classes and she worked hard to increase flexible seating options.

Madison is a great example of teachers everywhere working to show up to do good on behalf of the students they serve. She spent time naming her beliefs and ways they show up or can show up in her practice. What a joy to support Madison and watch students' motivation and engagement soar as changes were put into place to increase students' thinking and doing time.

Studying Instructional Time Protocol

Directions: If you want to study the ways instructional time is being used across an instructional block, use this multi-step process to collect data to inform decision-making. First, consider your role:
- **If you are a teacher,** you can study how you are using time by using a clock/watch and taking note of the types of instructional designs occurring across your block or period. You can record using audio or video. You can also ask a colleague to help you study instructional time through observation and note-taking.
- **If you are an instructional coach or administrator,** you can study how teachers are using time by creating shared agreements with teachers around what, when, where, why, and how time will be studied and the implications for work going forward. A note of caution that studying time without a shared agreement with teachers may feel evaluative, defeating the original intent.

Materials:
- *Studying Instructional Time* Template
- 2 highlighters, different colors
- Clock/watch
- Clipboard (optional)

Time: Length of instructional block or period and 10-15 reflection time afterward

Audience: Teachers, support staff, instructional coaches, administrator

Step 1: Schedule a time to study an instructional block.

Step 2: At the beginning of the instructional block, use a clock/watch to note the time. Use asset-based language to describe what is happening across the classroom. Continue to take note of observations until the end of the block.

Step 3: Review your observational notes. Use a highlighter to mark the places across the instructional block where the teacher was doing the majority of the work. For example, highlight the time used for a minilesson or direct instruction, Then, using a different highlighter, mark the places across the instructional block where the students were doing the majority of the work.

Note: If the teacher and students share the instructional time, such as a shared reading or guided practice, split the number of minutes and give half to the teacher and half to the students.

Step 4: Through conversation and collaboration, analyze and reflect on the ways instructional time is being used. Ask questions such as:
- How is the time allotted being used?
- Who "owns" the majority of the learning time?
   - What percentage of time does the teacher have?
   - What percentage of time do students have?

Step 5: Through reflection, name the implications for your work going forward? Based on the findings, ask:
- Are there changes I would like to make regarding the use of time during the instructional block?
- What if I/we shortened the minilesson or direct teaching time?
- What if I/we increased the time allotted for student work time?
- Can I make any desired changes on my own or do I need the support from my colleagues and/or administrator?

Studying Instructional Time Note Catcher

Time	What is Happening Across the Classroom (Describe what is happening using asset-based language)

Planning for Student Work Protocol

Directions: We know that when we keep minilessons or direct instruction time short, it gives more time for students to work independently, in small groups or one-on-one with the teacher. Try out this step-by-step process for planning that prioritizes student work time over teacher talk time.

Materials: Provide a copy of one of the *Lesson Planning Templates* for each participant

Time: 30-45 minutes (planning times may vary)

Audience: Teachers, support staff, instructional coaches, administrators

Step 1: Name the amount of time you have for your instructional block (Ex. 60 minutes.) Then, divide up the time so that you give approximately 1/3 to the teacher and 2/3 to the students (Ex. 20 minutes for the teacher, 40 minutes for the students.)

Step 2: Plan instruction for several days, keeping this time allotment in mind.

Step 3: Put your plans into action across several days, making adjustments as needed.

Step 4: Reflect on your plans and ask:
- Did students have approximately 2/3 of the learning time across several days to do the work?
    - What worked? What were the benefits?
    - What's clunky? What didn't feel quite right?
- Was the time I used to teach (minilessons or direct teaching time) enough to accomplish my goals?
    - If not, why not?
    - What could I adjust to make it better?

Lesson Planning Template #1

Time (# of minutes)	What	Instructional Plans
1/3 of the total time	Minilesson / Direct Teaching	
2/3 of the total time	Student Work Time	

Lesson Planning Template #2

If you plan instruction using the Workshop Model, you might consider using this planning template.

Time (# of minutes)	What	Instructional Plans
1/3 of the total time	Kick-off	
	Minilesson / Direct Teaching	
2/3 of the total time	Student Work Time	
If the teacher is sharing, add this time to the teacher minutes. If students are sharing, add this time to the student minutes.	Share out / Debrief	

PROTOCOL

Looking at Student Work Protocol

Directions: When we look across student work, it gives us data, or intel, for what students know, can do, and what they need next. Use the these steps to guide your instructional plans.

Materials:
- Process-oriented student work
- Sticky-notes, different colors (any size)

Time: 20-30 minutes

Audience: Teachers, support staff, instructional coaches, administrators

Step 1: Assign and collect process-oriented student work. A reminder that mid-process work, formative versus summative, is a great way to begin looking at student work (Ex. student writing such as drafts and revisions, student work that shows how ideas are evolving, student explanations that uncover the thinking to support the answer.)

Step 2: During a planning period, PLC meeting, or Team Meeting, participants gather to look at student work. Keep the following in mind:

Teachers or teams can look at...	Student work can...
• Their own students' work • Student work from another class • The same work at the same time • Different work at the same time • Student work (same or different) individually and then get together to talk about their observations, interpretations, and implications for their work • A randomly selected subset of student work (especially if teachers are just learning to look at student work)	• Include student names • Be anonymous • Be drafty, unfinished or unpolished • Be formative or summative • Be a portion of the total work (Ex. introduction of an essay versus the whole essay)

Set yourself up for success by avoiding some pitfalls when looking at student work. Be cautious when selecting student work samples such as:

Type of Student Work	What Makes It Tricky?	What Can We Do About It?
Multi-page pieces of work	Too much and too long makes it overwhelming to create a focus for instruction	Break it apart, select one part of the work to focus on that has the biggest impact on a focus for instruction
Multiple choice, bubble in responses	Student thinking behind responses is unknown	Select a few high-leverage multiple choice questions and ask students to write about their thinking/process. They could answer these types of questions: • How did you solve it? • What makes you believe this is the best response? • Tell me why. • Explain what you are thinking.
Projects	Too many requirements and/or sections	• Co-construct shared agreements with students ahead of time by naming "what counts." • This can be done in the form of a co-constructed rubric or a "Must Do" vs. "Can Do" checklist.

| Group Work | It can be hard to tell what students contributed individually and/or collaboratively, making students' understandings and misconceptions hard to name | • First, meet with students in the group for a mid-process check-in and ask:
  ○ How are things going?
  ○ What is working? What is clunky?
  ○ What are your big take-aways in your new learning? What is confusing?
• Then, provide students with an opportunity to reflect on the whole group work experience through writing by asking questions such as:
  ○ What did you learn about the content, about yourself, and about working with others that are worth using in the future?
  ○ Is there anything about this project or process that you would change in the future?
  ○ What, if anything, should I know that you have not already shared? |

Step 3: Look across the student work, select one set of questions, and ask:

Asset-Based Questions	Clearing up Confusion or Misunderstandings Questions	Creating a Focus for Instruction Questions
• What assets can be found in the work? • What can students do well (independently or with some support)? • What are our next steps?	• Where did students get stuck? • What are our theories about what caused confusion/misunderstanding? • What are our next steps?	• What does the whole class need next? • What do small groups of students need next? • What do individual students need next?

Closing the Gap Between Beliefs and Practices Protocol

Directions: Pick one focus area (education, learning, formative assessment, motivation and engagement, culturally responsive practices, etc.) and provide time for participants to name their beliefs and how those beliefs show up in their practice. Suggest that they create a fast draft of beliefs, getting ideas down on paper versus wordsmithing a final version.

Materials: Notebook, paper, or computer and a writing tool or provide a copy of the *Beliefs & Practices* Template.

Time: 20-30 minutes

Audience: Teachers, support staff, instructional coaches, administrators

Step 1: Create a two-column chart or provide a copy of the *Beliefs & Practices* Template. Give participants 10-15 minutes to create a first draft of their beliefs and practices.

Step 2: Break participants into pairs or trios so that they can share beliefs and practices with others. Remind them that they can lend and borrow ideas from one another to add or revise their beliefs and practices if they desire.

Step 3: Encourage participants to take a close look at their list of beliefs and practices. Ask:

Is there one or two beliefs and practices that you would like to:
- Add something new to your routines and practices?
- Do something more often?
- Do something differently?
- Do something less often?
- Eliminate something from your routines and practices?

Step 4: Once participants self-identify beliefs and practices that they want to make some changes to, they can use the *Beliefs, Practices & Making Changes* Template to name the desired actions.

Step 5: After participants have had the opportunity to put their beliefs, practices, and changes into action for a few weeks, find opportunities for them to share out any reflections. Invite them to share insights about any of the following questions:
- What changes did you try to make? Was it beneficial and if so, how?
- What did you notice about how your practices changed or did not change? Explain why you believe this to be the case.
- Did your actions strengthen, weaken, or modify your beliefs and/or practices? Is so, how and why?
- Have you added any beliefs and/or practices to your chart? If so, what are they?

Beliefs & Practices Template

This I Believe (What do you believe?)	I Will (How does this show up in your work?)

Beliefs, Practices & Making Changes Template

This I Believe (What do you believe?)	I Will (How does this show up in your work?)	Making Changes (How would you like to make a change?)

Teacher Self-Reflection Protocol: Increasing Students' Thinking and Doing Time

Directions: The support structures we provide to students are multi-faceted. Take time to self-reflect using the questions as a guide.

Teacher Self-Reflection: Increasing Students' Thinking and Doing Time

Question	Self-Assessment					What do you need next? What are your next steps?
I/we have taken stock of how the allotted instructional time is being used across the class period and school day, week, and year.	Seldom		Some of the time		Most of the time	
	1	2	3	4	5	
I/we can compare the amount of teacher talk time with the amount of student thinking and doing time.	Seldom		Some of the time		Most of the time	
	1	2	3	4	5	

Problem of Practice #4

What needs to happen to increase students' thinking and doing time? What do we learn when we compare the amount of teacher talk time with the amount of student thinking and doing time? List steps or bullet points to describe your perspective.

Increasing Students' Thinking & Doing Time	Comparing Teacher Talk Time with Student Talk Time

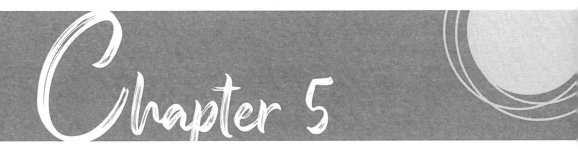

PROBLEM OF PRACTICE #5:
We need good instruction because that makes the best interventions.

It was not so long ago that I sat in a collaborative planning meeting, notebook, and favorite pen in hand, ready to jump right into learning about structures and routines for supporting students. Since I was new to this team, titled with a coaching role for classroom teachers and support staff, I spent a few weeks shadowing and observing the process. At the onset of the first meeting, there were pleasantries, of course. Soon after, the special education teacher, who was leading this meeting, flashed some student names with accompanying numbers onto a screen. Within minutes, some additional information was shared from the meeting attendees, one at a time. The details focused almost solely on the numerical data, interventions that had been employed, with a nod every so often toward student behaviors. Then, onto the next kiddo. By the time 30 minutes had passed, six different students and corresponding numerical data had been displayed and discussed. Also, instructional support decisions were put in place.

The principal described this meeting structure as *a well-oiled machine*. I could see why he described it that way — it was efficient in the sense that the team got through the kids on the list in the allotted time. The problem was, while the team was finishing up the last student, I was still thinking about the first student on the list. For the sake of example, we will call this student Maya. As the team was standing up, gathering materials, and getting ready to head back to their classrooms, I couldn't help but wonder:

- How many siblings does Maya have? And, where does she fall regarding birth order?
- What does Maya like to read for pleasure? What is currently in her book stack?
- On the day of the assessment that was discussed, when Maya's score

had taken a dip compared to other days, what did she have for breakfast? Was she her typical happy self or did something set her in an odd direction for the day? Did Maya self-select the text for the assessment or was it chosen for her?
- Who are her best buds? What did they like to do together?
- What does Maya do in her free time?
- Does Maya speak any other languages? What about her family members?
- What makes Maya laugh?
- Does Maya like to write?
- What does Maya consider as her strengths? Areas needing a lift?
- What types of instruction gets Maya moving?
- What types of intervention hadn't been successful and why?
- What does Maya's daily and weekly literacy journey look, sound, and feel like?
- How would Maya be described, from a whole-child perspective, by others? How would she describe herself?

What I was craving was a fuller picture of who Maya is as a person — beyond the numbers. Please don't get me wrong. The teachers around the table cared about their students and probably knew some of the answers to the questions I had jotted in my notebook. But, what I couldn't figure out was why this type of essential information was not shared about any of the students?

After two weeks of listening to this process, the pattern that emerged looked a little bit like an equation.

> Numerical data small **+** amount of qualitative data **=** structured support and placement decision-making

The process was efficient, according to the meeting participants who explained, "It is working better than it had in the past." Students were assessed regularly and provided support in three or six-week cycles, depending on what the team thought would be most beneficial for the student. The team worked hard to be swift and precise in their decision-making. In addition to an over-reliance on numerical data and an under-reliance on qualitative data, there were other key areas that I believed needed some attention. For example:
- Most of the interventions, or student supports, were provided in a pull-out, more restrictive setting.

- Most interventions were formulaic and did not necessarily match rituals and routines that fit naturally with the enacted curriculum. Instead, the team determined a "research-based intervention" to try for 3 weeks. Then, they would meet to discuss quantitative data. If it was successful, the student was "released" from intervention. If it was unsuccessful, the team selected a different "research-based intervention" for a new 3-week cycle.
- Successful, enduring Tier 1 instructional practices were rarely discussed. As a result, the idea of intervention as a *double dip* was often missing from the conversation. Also, it felt as though the instructional programming, prepared and delivered by the support team, was far different from Tier 1 classroom instruction.
- The percentage of students receiving support outside of Tier 1, the student's classroom, was high. Additionally, the number of students being referred to, and receiving special education services was on the rise.

EFFICIENT & EFFECTIVE

Efficiency, at the basic level, means performing or completing tasks without wasting time, energy, or materials. To be effective means accomplishing the desired goals or intended outcomes. The sweet spot is using them together — being efficient and effective in our efforts. Think about a simple example by imagining an upcoming presentation.

If I/we...	Then I/we could...	So that...
Want to share with staff the importance of and ways to build classroom community	• Think about what the audience already knows and what they need next • Gather talking points to turn into slides • Build in research to support our stance • Build in how-to, actionable steps that participants can use • Practice giving the presentation and make needed adjustments	We can build background knowledge, provide steps for, and inspire more classroom community building

Figure 5.1 If, Then, So Presentation Example.

Thinking through structures or initiatives using the *If-Then-So* process creates opportunities for a person or group to create actions more efficiently and effectively. Remember the data meeting structure I referenced? Here's one way to think about it using the *If-Then-So* process:

If I/we...	Then I/we could...	So that...
Make decisions and respond to students' academic, social, and physical needs in the least restrictive environment	• Discuss students' needs regularly and promptly • Use current, at-your-fingertips data • Respond to students' needs using Tier 1 instruction as our go-to • Pivot to new responses, if and when needed • Reflect on data, responses, and next steps	We ensure increasing ALL students' growth and success

Figure 5.2 If, Then, So Data Meeting Example.

When we use the *If-Then-So* process, we create a systematic way to consider new ideas, while honoring actions that might already be adding value, to be more efficient and effective in our efforts.

NAMING THE PROBLEM

Problem Of Practice #5: We Need Good Instruction Because that Makes the Best Interventions.

We need good instruction. We need good, solid, dependable, flexible, responsive instruction all of the time. Instruction is good when it takes into account the data we gain from knowing students academically, social-emotionally, and physically. By this, I mean, sizing up what we know or think we know about students' specific strengths and areas needing a lift from each of those areas. Doing so gives us a fuller picture of who students are and what they might need to grow.

The least restrictive environment for students is most often right in their classroom, working, and learning right next to their teacher and peers. In Mary Howard's Book, *RTI from All Sides: What Every Teacher Needs to Know* (2009), she shares insights about 3 rings in Tier 1: High Quality Curriculum, Differentiation, and Targeted Support. Howard explains, "The more expertly we attend to Tier 1, the more daily action there will be in *each* instructional ring. If each ring is filled with exemplary literacy practices, less outside support will be needed" (p. 35). When instructional designs and plans are created to meet all students' wants and needs in Tier 1, natural interventions are intentionally built-in. Those natural interventions are also known as good instruction. Students thrive when they are learning alongside their peers because of the social capital and stamina that this dynamic brings about. As a result, we need to design learning that harnesses good instruction because that makes the best interventions.

When students learn in the least restrictive environment, it is like activating all systems around the student — academic, social-emotional, and physical — to help maximize the learning inputs and outputs. Think about it this way:

Supports (Who can support the student?)	Inputs (What types of support can be provided?)	Student (What is the students' role?)	Outputs (What are the intended consequences with and for the student?)
• Classroom Teacher • Support Staff • Related Arts Teachers • Parents / Caregivers • Peers • Older Students (buddies or tutors)	• Make a list of the types of support the student needs and determine if it will be provided face-to-face or digitally • Determine the frequency, duration, and intensity of support	• Meet with the student to get his/her input about needs and wants • Discuss the students' roles and responsibilities for self-advocacy and active participation in learning	• What do we anticipate will happen as a result of the support? • How will we measure growth and development?

Figure 5.3 Supports, Inputs, Student, Outputs Example.

Unlike a machine model, this process is cyclical, not linear. As we make decisions with and for students, the process continues to inform itself. Districts, schools, and teams can use this process, efficiently and effectively, to outline support for students. Here are two examples:

MEET JEFFREY & FADUMA

Jeffrey is a second grader who is a self-proclaimed *non-reader*. Jeffrey's teachers know that is not true because he spends the first part of independent reading each day leafing through his favorite picture books. When given a long text such as a chapter book, Jeffrey has gusto launching into his reading but needs a lift sustaining and finishing a long piece of text. However, give Jeffrey a Lego building set meant for ages 10+ and he launches, sustains, and finishes his task, including reading all of the directions associated with building the design. Hoping to create the same type of stamina and success for him across content areas, Jeffrey's team came together to make a plan.

Supports (Who can support the student?)	Inputs (What types of support can be provided?)	Student (What is the students' role?)	Outputs (What are the intended consequences with and for the student?)
• Classroom Teacher • Small group reading with peer group (reading different books, written by the same author) • Student	• Teacher and student meet one-to-one, each day for several days (quick check-ins to talk about reading calendar) • Teacher and student continue to meet 2 times per week • Small group meets 2-3 times per week	• Stick to the plan outlined on the reading calendar co-created by the teacher and student • Actively participate in small group learning opportunities	• Student will finish a self-selected chapter book • Teacher will use reflection tools to gather data about student's perspectives • Student will increase reading volume by launching, sustaining, and finishing future chapter books

Figure 5.4 Supports, Inputs, Student, Outputs Jeffrey Example.

The key to Jeffrey's success is **his** role in this plan. That's because long-term growth and success require that:
1. Proximity is prioritized because working closely with others is a high-yield strategy.
2. Learners have autonomy and agency in decision-making.
3. Structures and routines are maximized to foster independence.

Faduma, a bilingual, cello-loving 5th grader, is a "book gobbler." Suggest a stack of reading material she might enjoy and before you can blink she has finished and is looking for more. Faduma loves period pieces. She just finished Avi's *True Confessions of Charlotte Doyle* and already has plans to reread it. Faduma's teachers explain that she is a delightful, helpful, easy student. They decided to meet because they worry that her growth trajectory may level off if her ideas and interests are not nurtured and fueled.

Supports (Who can support the student?)	Inputs (What types of support can be provided?)	Student (What is the students' role?)	Outputs (What are the intended consequences with and for the student?)
• Classroom Teacher • Buddy Classroom • Family/caregiver • Student	• Teacher and student meet to talk about opportunities for her to work with a younger buddy to read and write together 2x per week • Teacher, student and family/caregiver meet to discuss a volunteer program opportunity at the local Historical Society • Teacher and student meet to discuss ways the student can serve as a Book Ambassador for their 5th grade learning community	• Create a book stack to read with the younger buddy • Set up a time with family/caregiver to connect with the Historical Society • Meet with the 5th-grade teachers to co-design the vision for Book Ambassadors	• Student will share her love of books with a younger buddy • Student will learn how to connect with a local agency, learn about their needs and volunteer opportunities • Student will help co-create a Book Ambassador Program, which will include many students across the grades, to help foster literacy-rich environments across the school

Figure 5.5 Supports, Inputs, Student, Outputs Faduma Example.

Using Faduma's interests and passions was essential in giving her the lift she needed to grow. Because of the team's approach, Faduma:
- Shared lots of books with 3 different younger buddies
- Began volunteering at the local Historical Society and helped plan an interactive exhibit called *Tell Us Your Story*
- Joined the 5th-grade teachers and 5 other students to co-create the goals and first steps of the Book Ambassador Program

Jeffrey and Faduma did not need to receive support from a specialist to move forward. Neither needed a special education teacher nor a Gifted and Talented program. Instead, they both needed creative and collaborative problem solving from a supportive team. They both also needed to be an active participant in the problem-solving process. Most importantly, both Jeffrey and Faduma needed consistent and responsive instruction. Read on to learn about my beliefs about all students needing good instruction because that makes the best interventions.

THIS I BELIEVE

This I Believe (What do you believe?)	**I Will** (How does this show up in your work?)
Boosting knowledge, skills, and understandings through early literacy and numeracy initiatives gives students a "leg up" and has long-lasting impacts.	Create early intervention structures that fit naturally with the flow of content within the students' classroom and provide opportunities for on-the-spot formative assessment and responsive instruction.
Focusing on small-group learning opportunities across all grades and content areas is a necessary structure in meeting ALL students' needs.	Use on-going, strategic small group learning experiences to provide opportunities for personalized, differentiation.
Creating support structures and schedules that prioritize push-in versus pull-out, including planning time with and among all teachers involved in supporting students, is essential for students' success.	Prioritize student learning IN the students' regular or Tier 1 classroom setting to create learning opportunities in the least restrictive environment yielding the greatest results.
Developing curriculum that includes the use and study of students' identities creates holistic learning opportunities.	Develop units of study that allow ALL students to study themselves and others through culture, race, ethnicity, language or expression, family, and community.

Figure 5.6 This I Believe / I Will.

BRIDGING THE KNOWN TO THE NEW

I have been a long-time fan of Carol Ann Tomlinson's work. She helped birth the term "differentiation" and, in my opinion, put context to it, making it understandable and doable. Her decades of work in schools shifted mindsets to focus on students' rights for growth and development of educators' responsibilities in protecting those rights. In 2014, Tomlinson wrote a piece that has been pivotal in my work. Each fall, before I ramp up my work in schools, I get out an article she wrote which focuses on building a bridge between today's lesson and tomorrow's by using formative assessment as the guide. Tomlinson (2014) writes:

> Formative assessment is—or should be—the bridge or causeway between today's lesson and tomorrow's. Both its alignment with current content goals and its immediacy in providing insight about student understanding is crucial to helping teachers and students see how to make near-term adjustments so the progression of learning can proceed as it should.

I have kept this quote close to my work because it gets at the heart and purpose of our educational work. It's our job to create the bridge from day-to-day, week-to-week, unit-to-unit, and so on. When we use formative assessment — what students' produce to make their knowledge, skills, and understandings visible to others — we are better positioned to look closely at what kids bring to the table in service of their learning and growth. Then, we can create a mindset of using students' assets as a baseline. Using that data to create meaningful and purposeful learning opportunities gives us opportunities to support students' individual and collective needs and wants. When we bridge the known to the new, our well-planned, well-intentioned good instruction becomes the best intervention.

WHAT CAN WE DO ABOUT IT?

If we want to shift the mindset and focus on good instruction that makes the best intervention, we have to shift our focus to Tier 1 instruction. That means shoring up our practices in Tier 1 and using that instruction as our first line of defense in supporting ALL students. Each district has unique needs with varying resources which means that making this shift takes careful planning. However, there are three actions every district can take that will jumpstart the system.

1. Use 40+ years of research to back our decision-making with a focus on increasing reading and writing volume.
2. Create an early intervention initiative.
3. Ensure small group learning opportunities are a consistent structure for all grade levels and content areas.

INCREASING READING & WRITING VOLUME

For decades, Richard Allington has been standing up for kids. He believes, as do I, that good reading instruction does not cost a lot of money or time (Allington, 2002). Rather, it takes will and the know-how to arm kids with texts to read and opportunities to write and then get out of their way. Instead of supplanting good instruction with programs and an over-assessment stance,

Allington (2002) says we need to provide opportunities and support students in:
1. Reading what he/she wants to read.
2. Learning strategies for reading with accuracy.
3. Making meaning from their reading.
4. Writing about something personally meaningful.
5. Talking, sharing, discussing ideas from reading and writing with peers.
6. Learning alongside adults who read fluently.

When working with teachers and students, I often say, "Eyes on print. Eyes on print. Eyes on print," To me, it matters less what kiddos read as long as they are reading widely, deeply and across time. I also often say, "Pen to paper. Pen to paper. Pen to paper," to get at the importance of writing widely, deeply and often. In our digital world, and depending on the audience, I might also try to bring home the same point by saying, "Fingers on keyboard. Fingers on keyboard. Fingers on keyboard," in hopes to inspire writing volume in whatever form reaches the student.

Increasing the volume of reading and writing at the secondary level is critical to prepare students for life after graduation. We can use Allington's (2002) research to extend to current times as well as extend the findings and apply the same foundational principles to reading and writing across content areas. Reading and writing regularly provides many life-long, positive inputs for learning. That's because when we read widely and deeply across content areas and grade levels, we:
- Get a taste of new or unfamiliar information that may pique our interests and nudge us to read and write more
- Build our background knowledge about a variety of subjects and topics
- Access language and ideas that we may otherwise miss
- Create opportunities for diverse conversations
- Inspire creativity and ingenuity
- Become equipped to read the world around us in thought-provoking ways

To take on those endeavors, we cannot wait until adulthood to build those rituals and routines. We must begin building this mindset beginning in the foundational years so that these same habits carry over into adulthood. Secondary content subject areas create a "read-the-world, know-the-world, impact-the-world" kind of atmosphere. About a decade ago, there was a big push to bulk up reading and writing in the content areas. For many, adding content (or perceived content) to an already packed curriculum rubbed secondary content teachers the wrong way. It wasn't that they didn't believe it wasn't a good idea. Rather, they just couldn't imagine how they would fit it in. Now, more than ever, teachers across content and grade levels have worked to look at utilizing reading and writing as not "one more thing," but a vehicle for their "thing."

For example, in a tenth-grade geometry class, a teacher might ask students to find the area of a quadrilateral and then follow up by explaining what they did or how they solved for the answer. In this case, the student reports a number representing the area and then his/her process for figuring it out. Or, in an Earth Science course, students who are studying clouds might be asked a few multiple-choice questions about clouds and then asked to write why clouds can move if they are filled with water vapor. By using a singular form of summative assessment, such as multiple-choice questions, it is easy to fall into the trap of who got it *right* and who got it *wrong*. But, when students have to go a step further and explain their thinking, we might learn more about their understanding of condensation and buoyancy, which we may otherwise miss.

The key to all of this is having a district, building, or team-wide conversation about the different ways students will be engaged in meaningful reading and writing learning opportunities across the day, across classes, and courses. This is less about assigned reading and required writing prompts and more about the intentional design and attention to boosting reading and writing volume that matters.

This can be accomplished through planning — by analyzing the number of minutes students have for literacy and creating a shared agreement about how many of those minutes students will spend increasing their reading and writing volume. Here is a planning grid that can be used to go from ideas to actions:

How many minutes will students have to read and write across the week?	How will we know if it is working? What evidence of impact will we authentically collect or measure?	What is their role(s) in this work? (students)	What is our role(s) in this work? (adults)

Figure 5.6 Analyzing Instructional Minutes.

Elementary Example

How many minutes will students have to read and write across the week?	How will we know if it is working? What evidence of impact will we authentically collect or measure?	What is their role(s) in this work? (students)	What is our role(s) in this work? (adults)
Across the week, students have independent reading opportunities during the following content/times: • Reading Workshop 50 minutes per day • Social Studies or Science 50 minutes every other day • Music 50 minutes, 2 times per week Across the week, students have shared reading or other literacy opportunities during the following content/times: • Read aloud 15 minutes each day • Math literacies (reading math problems) 50 minutes each day • At home reading experiences 20 minutes each day	Reading Calendars • Text types read • Minutes read • Thoughts, goals, and reflections about reading Small-Group Reading Share Outs • Opportunities to share new books, new authors, new learnings Build Your Stack • Visit classroom, school and community library to add to personal Build Your Stack collections One-to-One Conferring • Student-to-Student • Teacher-to-student	• Keep track of reading using Reading Calendars • Actively participate in small group sharing experiences • Adding texts to personal Build Your Stack collections • Sign up for a teacher or peer conference	• Set up structures for Reading Calendars and create flexible options if students want or need to use them differently • Create time and space across the week for students to meet in small groups • Make sure students have access to library systems • Create time and space across the week for students to meet 1:1

Figure 5.7 Analyzing Instructional Minutes Elementary Example.

Secondary Example

How many minutes will students have to read and write across the week?	How will we know if it is working? What evidence of impact will we authentically collect or measure?	What is their role(s) in this work? (students)	What is our role(s) in this work? (adults)
Across a week, a freshman has opportunities for reading across content areas in the following ways: English Class: 100 minutes World Cultures: 70 minutes Biology: 50 minutes Electives: 30 minutes	English Class • Student reading recommendations posted on the Digital Bookshelf • Student and teacher initiated book clubs • "Novel or Text Set Every Two Weeks" initiative World Cultures • Socratic Seminar discussions and notes Biology • Synthesis of lab notes and readings Electives • Real-world demonstration of reading across the content such as music performances, speaking engagements in a foreign language, application of how-to's in studio art	• Participating in and contributing to digital and in-person experiences for sharing	• Creating time and space for students to contribute and share, both digitally and in-person

Figure 5.8 Analyzing Instructional Minutes Secondary Example.

Make a plan that honors time for students to increase their reading and writing time and students will grow. Building a culture of literacy is not an easy task. Not because people do not believe in it, but because it's hard, messy work. You have to give it time to take root, nurture it as it grows, and celebrate the results. Oh, and then, you have to go at it again...giving the same time and importance to it year after year because lifelong literacy is not a thing that we achieve in one year. When I work with districts and teachers I say, "Change is a process, not an event." I learned that from my friend and colleague, Donna Santman. In our work together, we reminded one another that the process over end product is what makes our work a beautiful, living, dynamic response to those we serve. Lifelong literacy is no different. Whether we are talking about students or adults, it is a journey. It is something we do now...and continue to do the rest of our lives, which includes the time we spend in school.

EARLY INTERVENTION

Early intervention is not a new idea. The concept of supporting students in the early grades has been around for several decades. I believe what has changed over the years is how students receive support. In many ways, we went from loose support without much structure to rigid support tied to lockstep decision-making. Creating an early intervention initiative that coalesces with and within Tier 1 curriculum and instruction helps us find the right balance. That's because a cohesive instructional design is NOT one that has one thing going on in one place and another thing going on in another place. Instead, both places are in sync with one another — shared vision, shared practices, shared goals. I have supported several school districts where I have helped shape an early intervention program. Since the spirit behind these initiatives is to catch kids and lift them -- helping them develop needed knowledge, skills, and understandings — calling them Early Lift Initiatives is appropriate. In some districts, we called them *K Lift* because the emphasis was on kindergarten. In other districts, there was an *Early Literacy Lift* because the focus was on K-3. And, yet, in another district, there was an *Intermediate Lift Initiative* because the focus was on grades 4-6. Regardless of district or title of the program, the goal was the same...giving students what they need to move toward and reach success.

Developing Early Lift Initiatives
1. Gather the right people and create a shared vision for what early intervention is and what it is not.

2. Work in cycles or rounds.
3. Meet again as a whole team to reflect and create the next steps.

Early Intervention Planning Process Example

This is an example of a planning process that you can use to design early intervention. This is a tweaked version of the protocol that is included at the end of the chapter.

Step 1:

Grades K-3 Classroom teachers, Tier 2 Reading teachers, Special Education teacher

- Create beliefs about early intervention, specifically good instruction as a means of intervention
- Outline foundational reading, writing, speaking & listening, and language knowledge, skills, and understanding, and create a natural learning progression
- Divide up foundational skills and create interactive, hands-on learning experiences that can be used for whole class, small groups or 1:1 instruction
- Create instructional teams to work alongside one another in the classroom during the literacy block (Ex. 1 classroom teacher + 1 Tier 2 reading teacher OR 1 classroom teacher + speech therapist OR 1 classroom teacher + 1 special education teacher + 1 school counselor)
- Focus on the instructional setting by prioritizing the least restrictive environment for all students

Step 2:

- Create cycles or rounds of instruction/intervention (1 and 2-week rotations)

- Everyone on the instructional team pushes into the Tier 1 classroom

- Mid-way through the cycle or round, teachers pause and reflect
    - What's working?
    - What's clunky?
    - Do we need to pivot?
- At the end of the cycle or round, teachers pause and reflect
    - What's working?
    - What's clunky?
    - Do students need more time and experience or are we ready to move on?
- Make plans for and launch the next cycle or round of instruction/intervention

Step 3:

- After several cycles or rounds OR at a time pre-determined by the team (Ex. at the end of the first quarter)

- What worked? What should we do more of?
- What was clunky? What should we change or do less of?
- What had the biggest take-away for student growth?
- What had the smallest take-away for student growth?
- Based on the results, what are our next steps? Who still needs support with the current content? Who is ready to move forward?

SMALL GROUP LEARNING

Small group learning has been a tried and true measure for many decades. However, it has often been reserved for younger students (in grades K-2) or for those students who are struggling or showing content weaknesses. When we utilize the small group structure, we prioritize proximity — getting up close to students' thinking and their work — as a guide to instruct, differentiate, and intervene. Small group instruction is a high-leverage move that should be an on-going, educational constant for all grade levels, for all content areas, and all students. Some key components include:

- Small groups are small — they can be pairs, trios, or groups of 4-6
- Students engage in meaningful and purposeful texts that he/she chooses
- Students have access to high quality, engaging, meaningful, and culturally responsive texts.
- Small groups can be teacher-led, student-led or a combination of both

Some considerations for launching and sustaining small group learning:
- Create a plan for all students to engage in small group learning opportunities. Plans may vary depending on building focus, grade level or classroom curriculum, and individual students' needs and wants.
- Ensure small group learning experiences are dynamic, switching them up regularly. Instead of creating static groups that meet on a specific day of the week and are tied to a reading level, consider flexible groups based on interests, passions, and inquiries. A reminder that students in a small group can:

- Read the same texts or different texts
- Read, write, discuss, and/or share
- Meet daily or create a schedule for when they will meet across a week.
- Meet with or without the teacher present

A reminder that teachers can:
- Use student interest surveys to create or co-create small groups
- Lean in and listen in as a small group is meeting and kidwatch / take anecdotal notes
- Join in as a participant
- Join in as a facilitator
- Be present for all or part of the small group experience

- Design small group experiences where students read different text types. Some examples include:
  - Novels
  - Picture books
  - Magazine and newspaper articles
  - Blogs and websites
  - Infographics
  - Short stories
- Create opportunities for students to curate texts for themselves and others to read. Students can:
  - Curate texts for themselves
  - Curate texts for other members in their small group
  - Curate texts for members in other small groups

To jump start planning for small group learning, try brainstorming ideas using this template:

Reasons for Grouping	What is the focus?	What does small group learning look, sound, and feel like?
Building Focus		
Grade Band / Grade Level		
Classroom / Individual Students		

Figure 5.9 Jump Start Planning for Small Group Learning.

Here is an example of a way this can look using grade-level bands.

Who	What is the focus?	What does small group learning look, sound, and feel like?
K-1	Guided Reading • Focus on skills & strategies • Mostly grouped by reading level	• Led by a teacher • Active student engagement and participation
2-5	Flexible Small Groups • Focus on reading widely and deeply • Rarely grouped by level • Honors student choice • Builds independence • Focus on all content areas, including integrated units	• Led by teacher and/or students • Teacher may lean in to listen or join in to participate/lead • Students may meet without the teacher present
6-8	Flexible Small Groups • Focus on reading widely and deeply • Group by interest and background knowledge instead of reading level • Honors student choice • Builds independence • Focus on all content areas, including integrated units	• Led by teacher and/or students • Teacher may lean in to listen or join in to model and ask questions • Students may meet without the teacher • More emphasis is on student's developing their reading assignments and pacing

9-12	Flexible Small Groups • Focus on reading widely and deeply • Rarely grouped by level • Honors student choice • Builds independence • Focus on all content areas, including integrated units • Might include students meeting outside of the school day when applicable	• Led by teacher and/or students • Teacher may lean in to listen or join in to participate/lead • Students may meet without the teacher • More emphasis is on student's developing their reading assignments and pacing • Students may agree to invite someone from outside the small group to join in for some/all of the work (Ex. invite a guest speaker or guest reader to join)

Figure 5.10 Jump Start Planning for Small Group Learning Grade-Level Bands.

For more about small group learning experiences, reference my book called *What Are You Grouping For?, Grades 3-8: How to Guide Small Groups Based on Readers, Not the Book* (Wright & Hoonan, 2019).

CREATE CULTURALLY RESPONSIVE LEARNING OPPORTUNITIES

We must develop curriculum and create learning opportunities that include the use and study of students' identities — the study of self and others through culture, race, ethnicity, language or expression, family and community. Gloria Ladson-Billings introduced the idea of culturally responsive teaching. She believed that when we teach with a culturally responsive pedagogy, there is a "commitment to collective empowerment where students experience success, develop cultural competence and a critical consciousness through which they challenge the status quo of the current social order" (Ladson-Billings, 1995). Some learning opportunities that focus on diversity, identities, and experiences of all students include:
- Studying family histories and sharing them with others
- Making connections between historical events with current day events, particularly as they relate to students' cultures, languages, and life experiences

- Relating content and developing lessons that include or consider students' interests, habits, and passions
- Creating culturally relevant word problems for math, linking ideas to students' interests and referencing diverse cultures
- Including diverse guest speakers to engage, educate and motivate all students
- Infusing multi-media that positively depicts a range of cultures and backgrounds
- Eliminating "one size fits all" experiences to ensure each students' needs and wants are prioritized

When we lean on the 40+ years of literacy research to guide our decision-making, create opportunities for increasing early interventions, and prioritize small group learning opportunities for all students, we have a greater chance of designing learning where the best interventions are simply good instruction.

If-Then-So Process Protocol

Directions: Create a three-column chart using the example below as a reference. This process can be completed independently or collaboratively.

Step 1: Name an *If I/we* statement and write it in the left column.

Step 2: Based on the desired goal or action, name an *Then I/we* statement, that can be taken to accomplish the goal and write it in the middle column.

Step 3: Name the intended consequences or outcomes, *So that* statement, that will result from this work and write it in the right column.

Step 4: Put the ideas into action.

Step 5: Meet to reflect and consider:
- Did our actions create the intended results? Why or why not?
- Based on what we know now, what are our next steps?

If-Then-So Template

If I/we...	Then I/we could...	So that...

Least Restrictive Environment Protocol

Directions: Create a four-column chart using the example below as a reference.

Time: 20-30 minutes

Audience: Teachers and support staff (and other stakeholders as needed)

Step 1: Schedule a meeting. Invite team members/stakeholders who know or support the respective student and/or classroom.

Step 2: Brainstorm ideas for each column in the chart.

Step 3: Looking across the chart, highlight the highest leverage moves to try first.

Step 4: Determine how long the high leverage moves will be put into action before coming back together to reflect. Put the next meeting date on the calendar before the close of this meeting. Reminder: This is a dynamic process with lots of input and moving parts. If anyone from the team feels the need to meet sooner, formally or informally, encourage team members to initiate the process to keep the work moving forward. In other words, if changes need to be made to support students, there is no reason to wait for the scheduled meeting.

Step 5: Make the plan accessible to all stakeholders.

Inputs & Outputs Planning Template

Supports (Who can support the student?)	**Inputs** (What types of support can be provided?)	**Student** (What is the students' role?)	**Outputs** (What are the intended consequences with and for the student?)

Increasing Reading and Writing Volume Protocol

Directions: Turn your ideas about increasing reading and writing volume into actions by making a fast draft plan for students. This can be completed independently or collaboratively.

Time: 10-15 minutes

Audience: Teachers and support staff (and other stakeholders as needed)

Step 1: Make plans for increasing students' reading and writing volume by using the headings in the template to guide your planning.

Step 2: Put plans into action for 2-3 weeks. Use this time to collect data about students' collective and individual reading and writing volume based on the plans you created.

Step 3: After 2-3 weeks (or as needed/wanted) meet briefly (5-10 minutes) to share findings. Ask:
- What have you noticed about students' reading and writing volumes?
- What is making the biggest impact?
- What are you wondering?
- Should we make any changes based on what we have learned?
  - What does the whole group need?
  - What do small groups need?
  - What do individual students need?

Analyzing Instructional Minutes Template

How many minutes will students have to read and write across the week?	How will we know if it is working? What evidence of impact will we authentically collect or measure?	What is their role(s) in this work? (students)	What is our role(s) in this work? (adults)

Early Intervention Planning Protocol

Directions: Create a five-column chart using the example as a reference.

Step 1: Schedule a meeting. Invite grade level team members and support staff (specialists, school counselors, etc.).

Step 2: Remind team members that this protocol is focused on creating an all-hands-on-deck, push-in model approach to support.

Step 3: Using the planning template, outline the structure of support. Determine, how will we support students through:
- Whole group instruction (minilessons or shared experiences)
- Small group instruction (teacher-led, student-led, or a combination of both)
- One-to-one (teacher to student)

Note: You can plan one quarter/month at a time OR the whole year.

Step 4: Using the planning template, outline the academic content. Ask:
- What content will be taught?
- What learning opportunities will students experience?
- What instructional resources will be used or needed?

Note: You can plan one quarter/month at a time OR the whole year.

Step 5: After each quarter/month, pause and reflect.
- What's working?
- What's clunky?
- What do we need to increase, decrease, or change in some way?
- Based on our reflections and data, what are our next steps?

Early Intervention Planning Template

	September	**October-December**	**January-March**	**April-June**
Structure of Support Whole Group Small Group 1:1				
Academic Content What content will be taught? What learning opportunities will students experience? What instructional resources will be used or needed?				

Teacher Self-Reflection Protocol: Good Instruction Makes the Best Interventions

Directions: The support structures we provide to students are multi-faceted. Take time to self-reflect using the questions as a guide.

Teacher Self-Reflection: Good Instruction Makes the Best Interventions

Question	Self-Assessment					What do you need next? What are your next steps?
I/we can determine if students are learning in the least restrictive environment based on their individual needs and wants.	Seldom 1	2	Some of the time 3	4	Most of the time 5	
I/we can size up if instructional designs and plans are created to meet all students' wants and needs.	Seldom 1	2	Some of the time 3	4	Most of the time 5	
I/we can design learning that harnesses good instruction because that makes the best interventions.	Seldom 1	2	Some of the time 3	4	Most of the time 5	

PROTOCOL

Problem of Practice #5

PROTOCOL

What needs to happen to ensure students are learning in the least restrictive environment? What do we learn when we create instructional designs and plans to meet all students' wants and needs? How can we ensure that we design learning that harnesses good instruction because that makes the best interventions? List steps or bullet points to describe your perspective.

Least Restrictive Environment	Instructional Designs & Plans to Meet Students' Wants & Needs	Good Instruction Makes the Best Interventions

Chapter 6

CLOSING THE KNOWING-NAMING-DOING GAP

Not long ago, I had the pleasure of coaching a group of amazing elementary and middle school teachers who were working on a district inquiry committee, focused on naming and using enduring practices to support student growth. This committee was also focused on using reflection and study to shake things up a bit. Admittedly, they explained that while their actions were well-intentioned, their support structures did not always create immediate and desired results. Through reflection, they shared that their partnerships and relationships with students and families were on steroids (in a healthy, productive way!), but they wondered if their instructional and intervention responses were too complicated which resulted in limited results.

Because this team had a collaborative, reflective mindset, I suggested a protocol to dissect their practices, diagnose the root of the issue, and determine next steps. Here's the protocol we used:

Directions: Within your small group, jot down ideas to the following questions. Do not wordsmith or overthink your answers, just jot what comes out of your collaborative brainstorm.

- **DISSECT:** What are your top 3-5 go-to instructional and intervention responses that you use with students?
- **DIAGNOSE:** Of your top 3-5 responses, note the actions that yield the biggest impact. Select as many or few as you want.
- **DETERMINE:** Based on your diagnosis, determine the next steps.
    - What will you keep the same?
    - What will you change?
        - What will you add or increase?
        - What will you eliminate or decrease?

Various grade level teams gave it a go and the following chart provides some examples of their responses:

Teacher Grade Level Department School	Dissect	Diagnose	Determine
Grade 2	• Guided Reading • Running Records • Strategy Minilessons • Meeting with students 1:1	• Running Records • Meeting with students 1:1	• Increase use of Running Records and make specific, intentional plans around that data
Grade 5	• Developmental Reading Assessments • Strategy Groups • Free Writes • Silent Sustained Reading (2 times per week) • 1:1 Reading and Writing Conferences	• Free Writes • Silent Sustained Reading	• Increasing the amount of time and days students can Free Write and choose Silent Sustained Reading using a Menu of Options during independent work time • NEW: Need to add in small group experiences (author studies, book clubs, genre studies)

Middle School Math Department	• Teacher-generated quizzes with collaborative student-generated responses • Meeting with students 1:1 during Academic Intervention Services period • Math independent study projects	• Teacher-generated quizzes with collaborative student-generated responses • Math independent study projects	• Ask students to share responsibility in generating quizzes (like a student-teacher team for the week) and increase the frequency of use • Decrease the use of math independent projects OR rethink them to make them more current and student-oriented • NEW: Revamp math Academic Intervention Services period (needs to be a school-wide discussion)

| High School Science Department | • Meet with the student to make sure he/she has access to the notes from class
• Invite the student to meet during before school office hours or possibly a study hall if schedules permit
• Recommend student to Child Study Team if things do not improve | • Meet with the student to make sure he/she has access to the notes from class | • Continue to meet with the student to make sure he/she has access to the notes from class
• NEW: When meeting with the student, find out more about how the student feels his/her work is going AND find out if there is anything this student needs.
• NEW: Restructure before school office hours to be included during the school day because mornings are not an optimal time for students and many do not take advantage of this time to get extra support. Since it is before school, it is not mandatory.
• NEW: Instead of recommending the student to the Child Study Team, first hold an internal department Child Study Team to come up with supports for the student. |

Figure 6.1 Dissect, Diagnose, Determine Grade-Level Examples.

Because the team was able to pause and reflect on current practices, they found opportunities for change and growth. When teachers feel safe and free of judgment, they typically work in honest, vulnerable ways, naming what's working and what's not. That can lead to really productive and positive measures, sometimes even evoking a call to action.

CLOSING THE KNOWING-NAMING-DOING GAP

Back in 2000, Jeffrey Pfeffer and Robert Sutton wrote a book called *The Knowing-Doing Gap*. At the time, I was working on my administrative licensure program at The Ohio State University, and this book was on the selected reading list for one of my classes. Admittedly, it was the first time in my career that I had thought about schools as a business. I remember having a little *aha moment* signifying my looking at schools through a wider lens. It was refreshing and exciting. This book challenged businesses to turn knowledge about how to improve into actions that produce measurable and desired results. Within the first few pages, I learned that if I did not use the knowledge I have and turn it into actions, my work might be filled with missed opportunities. The authors were talking about companies, customers and products. But, we used this text as a conversation starter about our companies (schools) and our customers (students) and our products (student growth, development, and success). This mind shift was pivotal in how I learned to approach challenges, hurdles, and curveballs in the learning communities I serve.

Many years have passed, and I have learned that for the work in schools another step is needed. If we want to attend to and close the knowing-doing gap, we have to pause in between and name what matters. Naming what matters makes us stop and dig into the WHY — why it matters in the first place. When we name something, we give it more power and more importance.

If we want to do good by the kids we serve, reflecting on our instructional practices and interventions is a must. Then, we can use our reflections to plan forward. Planning IS key to closing the *Knowing-Naming-Doing Gap*. When we know what to do and then name it, we have a better chance of doing what is needed to close the gap. A gap can exist in teacher know-how where teachers may need to learn or revisit practices that will yield greater student growth. This can also be focused on practices that a teacher knows, but does not employ as often. Or, the gap can exist in know-how when students have misunderstandings or misconceptions about content knowledge, skills, or understandings. Here are two examples:

Example #1: Closing the Teacher Knowing-Naming-Doing Gap

What are some instructional moves or teacher practices that you KNOW would benefit students? NAME the why behind them. Create steps for DOING them.

Knowing	Naming	Doing
Read-aloud or shared reading using short texts.	Read-aloud and/or shared reading provides: • A model for reading fluently • Metacognition (cracking our brains open for students) about ways we make meaning • Exposure to new and interesting texts that might fuel their choices during independent reading	1. Grab a short text that I love. 2. Share it with students by reading it aloud and displaying it under the document camera. 3. Stop (intentionally in places that may trip students up) and think aloud about my thinking and meaning-making. 4. Give students opportunities to read the same text or similar texts during independent reading.

Figure 6.2 Closing the Student Knowing-Naming-Doing Gap Example 1.

Example #2: Closing the Student Knowing-Naming-Doing Gap

What are the content, knowledge, skills, concepts, understandings, strategies, approaches, interactions, or tools that you KNOW would benefit students? NAME the why behind them. Create steps for DOING them.

Knowing	Naming	Doing
Connecting historical events and make thinking and understanding visible through writing and discussion.	Support students by: • Co-construct a timeline of historical events • Read texts that help students see the connections between historical events • Model ways to make thinking and understanding visible about the texts we read together and naming why this is an important practice	1. Use our digital timeline to collect events. 2. Read short texts about historical events. 3. While writing in front of students, use the thinking aloud strategy so that they know what is going on in my thinking process as we co-construct connections between and among the events. 4. Talk about different ways to make thinking and understanding visible. 5. Allow students to try out this same process in small groups or independently. 6. Allow students to share with others.

Figure 6.3 Closing the Student Knowing-Naming-Doing Gap Example 2.

Using the *Knowing-Naming-Doing* process paves the way for putting the DOING portion into action. If you anticipate that you might encounter hurdles or obstacles, you can jot those on the following chart. That way you take a proactive stance, naming a challenge ahead of time so that you can think through how you might address it before the experience. After taking action, you can name the hurdles or obstacles that you encountered and then reflect on the whole experience, guiding future instruction.

Knowing	Naming	Hurdles or Obstacles	Doing	Reflection

Figure 6.4 Knowing-Naming-Hurdles-Doing-Reflection Template.

The goal of the *Knowing-Naming-Doing Gap* protocol is two-fold. First, this process can become a cycle—using our reflections to loop back to KNOWING which informs the next steps. Second, this process should lead to greater student growth and success.

A CALL TO ACTION

Growth and development, for the whole child, is our goal. We do not have time, resources, or energy to waste. Our students deserve our attention, and they deserve our urgent responses that will nurture their needs and contribute to their overall growth. That is a big job that requires the development of and a commitment to using our knowledge to take action. There are many ways people and organizations can gather knowledge and turn it into actions. Some include:

- Set goals and name steps for reaching them.
- Ask others to observe, share, reflect and provide feedback.
- Create a priority list. Then, focus on what is important versus what is easy and feels good.
- Take responsibility for what is working and what is not. Use knowledge

from both to create steps forward.
- Just start.
- Make an accountability agreement with yourself and others using calendars and timelines. Somewhere in the midst of it, pause and reflect. Ask: Is the timeline still applicable or does it need to be adjusted?

Educational work is multifaceted, and the young people we serve deserve for us to act NOW. If a student is having trouble comprehending the texts he/she reads, we can't wait. If we want to decrease that gap, the time to act is NOW. If a student needs scaffolds built in to support her socially-emotional well-being, we can't wait four weeks to have an initial meeting to discuss observations and next steps. The time for that meeting is NOW.

Another way to use knowledge to act on a larger scale is to create a Call to Action or Manifesto. Maybe it is about EDUCATION. Maybe STUDENTS or LEARNING or ASSESSMENT. Or, maybe it'll be about the importance of PLAY or STUDENT VOICE. A teacher can create a Call to Action focused on his upcoming unit of study. A grade-level team can create a Call to Action about a year-long, animal rescue service project. A school can create a Call to Action about literacy. A district or community can create a Call to Action prioritizing the Arts. There is no one right way.

Here's an example focused on the power and empowerment in writing.

> We WRITE.
> We write to CELEBRATE.
> We write to INFORM.
> We write to NAME.
> We write to THINK.
> We write TO CONVINCE.
> We write to CONTRIBUTE.
> We write to INFLUENCE.
> We write to NOODLE.
> We write to MAKE SENSE OF.
> We write to REFLECT.
> We write to EMPOWER.
> We WRITE.
> ~JW, 2019

My friend and colleague, Isabel, wrote this beautiful Manifesto draft about peace.

> *"It isn't enough to talk about **peace**. One must believe in it. And it isn't enough to believe in it. One must work at it." ~ Eleanor Roosevelt*
>
> *I care deeply about peace...peace both in my personal world as well as in the world around me. Peace is important to my well-being — perhaps it is the hidden introvert inside of me that craves peace. Peace in the larger world outside of my home is critical to our experience on this planet. I am lucky enough to be a first-time grandmother and I am ever hopeful that my grandson, Jack, will grow up in a peaceful world. But, "isn't not enough to talk about peace. One must believe in it."*
>
> *I believe that making space for not only communication with one another but also for constructive conflict will offer us all some peace in the end. This is an odd juxtaposition, I know. But allowing time for all forms of communication with one another while also creating opportunities for safe discord is a clear way through the chaos we are living in peace. "It is not enough to believe in it [though]. One must work at it."*
>
> *I am committed to working for peace. That work starts with helping teachers make space for communication and conflict in their classrooms. And, in order for students to access this, teachers must first have this opportunity themselves. I am committed to helping teachers learn to better communicate with one another and work through conflict together...to create peace in our schools and for our children.*
> *~ Isabel, 2020*

My friend and colleague, Kristen, is a teacher who writes about play. Here's her thinking:

> **PLAY** By Kristen
>
> It is really hard for me to play. I am really great at stimulating play with books, props, questions, and conversation. But, actually sitting down and playing is hard. My four-year-old son can easily create entire worlds with his imagination. He will often say, "Mommy, play with me," but I do not know how. It is almost like that part of my brain has been destroyed. I can remember playing. I can remember taking inanimate objects and giving them a life and a voice. I can remember being so fully invested in my imagined stories and worlds, that when my mom would call me to eat dinner, it was hard for me to step back into reality.
>
> It is painful to wait for my children to find "something" to play. **The boredom that lingers before play can be excruciating.** As parents, my husband and I have made the decision to minimize screen time for our kids. So, we cannot "easily" distract our kids from their boredom with a TV show. Instead, we ALL have to embrace that waiting period before fully investing in play. Sometimes, it is really easy for our kids to dive into play, but other times it feels like there are hours of "what can I do" time before they engage in play. While this time can be torturous for me, I remind myself of how hard it is for me to play when Jett says, "Will you play with me?"
>
> Play is hard work. It is the work of creating from nothing.

When educators use what they learn from the *Knowing-Naming-Doing Gap* together with creating a Call to Action or Manifesto, the "what matters most" question is naturally answered. That's because it's natural to write about things that we care deeply about, not the things that don't matter as much in our daily work. When we decide something matters, we are much more willing to gather knowledge and intel around it, leading to greater opportunities to use that information to take action.

So, go ahead. Draft it!

WHAT'S OUR RESPONSE?

We know kids, teachers, instructional coaches, principals, families, and community members work to show up with their best foot forward. Schools have a way of bringing that out in people. That's because we want to nurture and support nations full of smart, kind, sophisticated, creative, passionate, thought-provoking, and thoughtful young people. The hope is that they continue to grow their smarts and develop their kindness and sophistication and creativity and passions and thought-provoking and thoughtful ways into adulthood. The educational world puts a big burden on us, but it's a burden that is welcomed because when we said we wanted to educate, it's exactly what we signed up for.

If you have reached the end of this book, I hope you feel of sense of empowerment because of increased opportunities to:
- Size up your beliefs and explore how they show up in your practice.
- Explore the history of RtI, including the policies that create inequalities, negative consequences, and roadblocks for students, particularly students of color who are underperforming, immigrants, and/or poor.
- Consider the steps necessary to create culturally responsive educational opportunities that are free of "handcuffs" created by mandates that put our most vulnerable students further at risk.
- Create processes to empower a shared responsibility to break out of the RtI box so that we can serve ALL students in meaningful, responsive ways.
- Name ways your learning community can advocate for and take advantage of increasing teacher autonomy and agency to make important decisions about instructional designs and plans that meet students' unique needs.
- Design child study teams that shine a light on students' assets versus deficits.
- Make instructional plans that increase students' thinking and doing time while decreasing the amount of teacher talk time.
- Prioritize student learning in the least restrictive environment, alongside their peers, to create opportunities for good instruction as the best interventions.

As you create systems and structures to support students, I hope you'll lean on your beliefs, your practices, and the protocols in this book as fuel for creating your Call to Action. And, the next time a plan is being made to support students' individual and collective needs, I'm hopeful that you will name students' assets as a go-to source for answering the important question, "What's our response?"

3 D's Protocol

Directions: Gather participants and explain that the goal of this protocol is to use reflections about current practices as an entry point for creating moves forward. Participants can work independently or collaboratively to jot ideas, but working collaboratively to make future decisions is important.

Step 1: Independently or collaboratively, jot down answers to these questions.
- DISSECT: What are your top 3-5 go-to instructional and intervention responses that you use with students?
- DIAGNOSE: Of your top 3-5 responses, note the actions that yield the biggest impact. Select as many or few as you want.

Step 2: Share your ideas with others. If applicable, record all ideas shared by participants.

Step 3: Collaboratively, use the ideas that have been shared to create the next steps.
- DETERMINE: Based on your diagnosis, determine the next steps.
  - What will you keep the same?
  - What will you change?
    - What will you add or increase?
    - What will you eliminate or decrease?

Step 4: Decide on a timeline for implementing the next steps.

Step 5: Calendarize the next meeting date so that participants can get together to share out and reflect on progress and changes made.

3 D's Template

Teacher Grade Level Department School	Dissect	Diagnose	Determine

PROTOCOL

Closing the Knowing-Naming-Doing Gap Protocol (Teachers)

Directions: Create a three-column chart using the example below as a reference.

Question: What are some instructional moves or teacher practices that you KNOW would benefit students? NAME the why behind them. Create steps for DOING them.

Closing the Knowing-Naming-Doing Gap Template (Teachers)

Knowing	Naming	Doing

Closing the Knowing-Naming-Doing Gap Protocol (Students)

Directions: Create a three-column chart using the example below as a reference.

Question: What are the content, knowledge, skills, concepts, understandings, strategies, approaches, interactions, or tools that you KNOW would benefit students? NAME the why behind them. Create steps for DOING them.

Closing the Knowing-Naming-Doing Gap Template (Students)

Knowing	Naming	Doing

Problem of Practice #6

Creating a Call to Action Protocol

Directions: There is no one right way to create a Call to Action or Manifesto. The most important aspect is to draft lots of ideas and know that it's okay if some of the ideas stay drafty for a while. This is an iterative process — as you draft and put ideas into action, you'll gain more insights into how and what you might add to your draft.

Step 1: Gather participants and determine if you will:
- Draft independently or collaboratively
- Create a Call to Action about the same topic/idea or different topics/ideas

Step 2: Draft your Call to Action. Make sure you date all of your drafts.

Step 3: Share your Call to Action with the group. Decide if you will continue drafting or create a final format.

Step 4: Personalize it, professionalize it, and publicize it! Ask:
- How will we personalize it?
- How will we professionalize it?
- How will we publicize it?

Step 5: Determine a date in the future where you will pause and reflect. Ask:
- How is our Call to Action showing up in our work?
- What are the current implications (positives and negatives) of our Call to Action? How do we know? What is our evidence?
- Does our Call to Action need to be revamped or revised?
- What are our next steps?

Teacher Self-Reflection Protocol: Closing the Knowing-Naming-Doing Gap

Directions: The support structures we provide to students are multi-faceted. Take time to self-reflect using the questions as a guide.

Teacher Self-Reflection: Closing the Knowing-Naming-Doing Gap

Question	Self-Assessment						What do you need next? What are your next steps?
I/we have created opportunities for thinking collaboratively and deeply about closing the knowing-naming-doing gap for ourselves.	Seldom		Some of the time		Most of the time		
	1	2	3	4	5		
I/we have created opportunities for thinking collaboratively and deeply about closing the knowing-naming-doing gap for students.	Seldom		Some of the time		Most of the time		
	1	2	3	4	5		
I/we can draft a Call to Action or Manifesto that is founded on our beliefs and designed to support our practices.	Seldom		Some of the time		Most of the time		
	1	2	3	4	5		

PROTOCOL

PROTOCOL

What needs to happen to close the *Knowing-Naming-Doing Gap* for teachers and students? How can drafting a Call to Action or Manifesto help honor our beliefs and support our practices? List steps or bullet points to describe your perspective.

Closing the *Knowing-Naming-Doing Gap* (Teachers)	Closing the *Knowing-Naming-Doing Gap* (Students)	Call to Action or Manifesto

References

Introduction

Bennett, Samantha. (2007). *That Workshop Book: New Systems and Structures for Classrooms That Read, Write, and Think*. Heinemann.

Clark, C.M. and Peterson, P.L. (1986) Teachers' Thought Processes. In: Wittrock, M.C., Ed., Handbook of Research on Teaching, 3rd Edition, Macmillan, New York, 255-296.

Fox, L., & Hemmeter, M. L. (2009). A program-wide model for supporting social emotional development and addressing challenging behavior in early childhood settings. In W. Sailor, G. Dunlap, G. Sugai, & R. Horner (Eds.), *Handbook of Positive Behavior Support* (pp. 177-202). New York, NY: Springer.

Chapter 1

Channing-Brown, A. (2020). Breaking all the rules with Kelly Hurst. Retrieved from https://austinchanning.substack.com/p/breaking-all-the-rules-with-kelly

Individuals with Disabilities Education Act, 20 U.S.C. § 1400 (2004).

Kendi, Ibram X. (2016). Why the academic achievement gap is a racist idea. Retrieved from www.aaihs.org/why-the-academic-achievement-gap-is-a-racist-idea/

Muhammad, G. (2019). *Cultivating genius: An equity framework for culturally and historically responsive literacy*. New York, NY: Scholastic.

Muhammad, G. (2020). Rethinking what matters: Incorporating anti-racism into teaching. Retrieved from www.languagemagazine.com/2020/05/19/rethinking-what-matters/

No Child Left Behind Act of 2001, 20 U.S.C. § 6319 (2008).

Silverstein, S. (1981). *A light in the attic*. New York, NY: Harper.

Chapter 2

Armstrong, T. (2012). First, discover their strengths. *Educational Leadership, 70*(2), 10–16.

Howard, Mary. (2012). *Good to Great Teaching: Focusing on the Literacy Work That Matters*. Heinemann.

Chapter 3

An asset-based approach to education: What it is and why it matters. (2018). Retrieved from http://teachereducation.steinhardt.nyu.edu/an-asset-based-approach-to-education-what-it-is-and-why-it-matters/

National Equity Project. (n.d.). *Educational equity definition*. Retrieved from www.nationalequityproject.org

Owocki, G., & Goodman, Y. M. (2002). *Kidwatching: Documenting children's literacy development*. Portsmouth, NH: Heinemann.

Rose, H. (2006). Asset-based development for child and youth care. *Reclaiming Children and Youth, 14*(4), 236-240. Retrieved from http://www.iicrd.org/sites/ default/files/resources/Asset-based_Development_for_child_and_youthcare_0.pdf

Wright, J., & Hoonan, B. (2019). *What are you grouping for? Grades 3-8: How to guide small groups based on readers - Not the book*. Corwin.

Chapter 4

Bennett, Samantha. (2007). *That Workshop Book: New Systems and Structures for Classrooms That Read, Write, and Think*. Heinemann.

Gallo, Carmine. (2015). *Talk like TED: The 9 public speaking secrets of the world's top minds*. New York, NY: St. Martin's Griffin,

Mills, H., & O'Keefe, T. (2015). Why beliefs matter. In E. O. Keene, & M. Glover, (Eds.), *The teacher you want to be: Essays about children, learning, and teaching* (pp. 31-49). Portsmouth, NH: Heinemann.

Wright, J. (2019, February 14). Everyone deserves a thinking partner! *Julie Wright Consulting*. Retrieved from www.juliewrightconsulting.com/blog/2019/2/14/everyone-deserves-a-thinking-partner.

Chapter 5

Allington, R. (2002). Every child, every day. *Educational Leadership, 69*(6), 10–15.

Howard, Mary. (2009). *RTI from All Sides: What Every Teacher Needs to*

Know. Heinemann.

Ladson-Billings, Gloria. (1995). But that's just good teaching! The case for culturally relevant pedagogy. *Theory into Practice, 34*(3), 159–165.
doi:10.1080/00405849509543675

Tomlinson, C. A. (2014). The bridge between today's lesson and tomorrow's. *Educational Leadership, 71*(6), 10–14.

Chapter 6

Pfeffer, J., & Sutton, R. I. (2000). *The knowing-doing gap.* Boston, MA: Harvard Business School Press.